## *Praise for*
## BE THE TRAIN

"If you're feeling stuck and tired of waiting for everything to fall into place, Selina Ringel's *Be the Train* is exactly what you need. Her compelling story will show you how to build unstoppable momentum and turn your dreams into reality. As an award-winning filmmaker who dared to do things her way, Selina offers practical tips and insights to help you take control of your future. Whether you're making your first film, launching a new career, or getting ready to take charge of your life, this book will ignite the fire within you to make it happen!"

—**MEL ROBBINS**, *New York Times* bestselling author and host of *The Mel Robbins Podcast*

"This book should be required reading at every film school. The cold email outreach chapter alone is worth the price of the book. But the real value is in the mindset she outlines. Inspiring. Motivational. Revolutionary. I'm on board the Selina train."

—**JOHN FITHIAN**, former CEO, National Association of Theatre Owners, and cofounder, The Fithian Group

"Selina is an undeniable force of nature. The advice she gives is invaluable for anyone who struggles with self-doubt or needs some practical guidance in this crazy industry. I wish I had read this book when I was starting out as a young filmmaker in Hollywood!"

—**AMY WANG**, writer of *Crazy Rich Asians 2*

"Even in my fourth decade as a professional filmmaker, I learned important essentials from Selina Ringel's *Be the Train*. The specificity of her advice, earned from her own hard work, speaks volumes about subjects like making genuine contacts, finding an agent and/or manager, production, distribution, rejection, resilience, failing better, and so much more. If you're looking for guidance, either as a rookie or as a refresher course for an old hand, this book is a must-read."

—**MICHAEL MINER**, cowriter, *Robocop*; director, *The Book of Stars*; and lecturer, University of California, Santa Barbara

"Selina Ringel has always had an infectious enthusiasm, which she's now sharing in her informative, inspiring, and frequently hilarious book, *Be the Train*! It's a must-read not just for aspiring and experienced filmmakers alike but for any creative soul chasing a dream and eager to start driving their own train."

—**DAN MIRVISH**, filmmaker, founder of Slamdance Film Festival, and author of *The Cheerful Subversive's Guide to Independent Filmmaking*

"*Be the Train* is a bold, no-nonsense guide for anyone ready to stop waiting and start building their success. Through her journey of making things happen—whether raising funds for films or forging unconventional paths—Selina shows that the keys to achieving your goals are to take action, embrace challenges, and create your own momentum. Her practical advice and fearless approach will inspire anyone looking to break the mold and take control of their career. If you're ready to stop waiting for opportunities and start making them, this book is for you."

—**DIANA LUNA,** executive director, National Association of Latino Independent Producers

"I'm only halfway through *Be the Train*, and I already feel inspired to produce my own movie! Selina Ringel's advice isn't just practical—it's a mindset shift that makes you believe you can make your film happen. A must-read for any aspiring filmmaker."

—**ANGELA GUICE,** Emmy-winning executive producer

"I can with absolute certainty say that I would never have directed my first feature if it hadn't been for a single phone call with my fellow Train, Selina Ringel. *Be the Train* is your phone call—actionable items from a passionate creator who brings positivity to a creative world that can often be riddled with self-doubt. The mindset she offers in this book will change your life and your ability to see yourself as a powerful force in the best, weirdest, most demanding industry in the world."

—**ANNA CAMPBELL,** director, actress, writer, and producer

"Selina's book not only motivates you to create your own brand but gives you the actual tools and tips on what steps you need to take to get you to where you want to go! This book is one you can read over and over again for inspiration. Having worked with Selina, I can confidently say she walks her talk. She is the Train, and she will inspire you to be one too."

—**KAELA CRAWFORD,** comedian and costar of *2 Moms, 1 Mic*

"In *Be the Train*, Selina Ringel reminds us of the innate power that we have to truly enjoy our lives. This book will give you all the tools you need to create your film, celebrate the process, and inspire others."

—**JORGE PEREZ,** author of *The Shut the Fu\*k Up Method*

"Selina's writing goes deep, dismantling the surface-level approach so many books take when it comes to making a feature film. While others hold back or engage in gatekeeping, she rips that wide open, sharing the raw, authentic truth of how she made it happen time and time again."

—**CAT DEL RE,** director and writer

you are
the TRAIN!
Love,

www.amplifypublishinggroup.com

*Be the Train: The Mindset and Tools You Need to Make Your First Feature Film*

©2025 Selina Ringel. All Rights Reserved. No part of this publication may be reproduced, stored in a retrieval system or transmitted in any form by any means electronic, mechanical, or photocopying, recording or otherwise without the permission of the author.

The views and opinions expressed in this book are solely those of the author. These views and opinions do not necessarily represent those of the publisher or staff. The publisher and the author assume no responsibility for errors, inaccuracies, omissions, or any other inconsistencies herein. All such instances are unintentional and the author's own.

**For more information, please contact:**
Amplify Publishing, an imprint of Amplify Publishing Group
620 Herndon Parkway, Suite 220
Herndon, VA 20170
info@amplifypublishing.com

Library of Congress Control Number: 2024927615

ISBN-13: 979-8-89138-599-3

Printed in the United States

A heartfelt thank-you to my family and friends for always supporting me, for giving me permission to take up space, and for helping me believe I am worthy of being the train.

To all my fellow trains who inspire me every day—you know who you are—I don't think you can; I know you can! Keep going.

To Matias and Camila, your joy, your energy, and your soul inspire me every day—because of you, I get to be me.

And to Dan—you are my rock, my best friend, a genius, and the only person I can imagine sharing this journey with.

*What a life.*

**The Mindset and Tools You Need to Make Your First Feature Film**

# BE THE TRAIN

an imprint of Amplify Publishing Group

# SELINA RINGEL

# Contents

INTRODUCTION
**HOW I BECAME THE TRAIN**    1

## PART I: ALL ABOARD!

CHAPTER 1
**WRITE YOUR OWN TICKET**    9

CHAPTER 2
**BE THE TRAIN**    13

CHAPTER 3
**DON'T GET STUCK AT THE STATION**    19

CHAPTER 4
**START THE JOURNEY WITH JOY**    23

CHAPTER 5
**PLAN YOUR ROUTE: WRITING**    27

CHAPTER 6
**EVERYONE YOU KNOW IS A POTENTIAL PASSENGER: CHARACTERS**    37

CHAPTER 7
**ASK EVERYONE TO JUMP IN: YOUR AUDIENCE WANTS TO RIDE WITH YOU**    41

CHAPTER 8
**BE THE ENGINE: PRODUCING**    45

CHAPTER 9
**BE THE ENGINEER: DIRECTING**    51

CHAPTER 10
**BE THE LEAD CAR: STARRING**    59

CHAPTER 11
**WEAR ALL THE HATS: WRITING, DIRECTING, AND STARRING**    65

## PART II: GETTING (AND STAYING) ON TRACK

CHAPTER 12
**SET AN ARRIVAL TIME** — 71

CHAPTER 13
**FIND A CONDUCTOR:
WHY A LINE PRODUCER MATTERS** — 77

CHAPTER 14
**DON'T STOP MOVING:
WHY PERFECTION DOESN'T
GET YOU ANYWHERE** — 83

CHAPTER 15
**KEEP THE RIDE SMOOTH:
STRUCTURING YOUR BUDGET** — 87

CHAPTER 16
**USE THE TRACKS YOU'VE GOT** — 91

CHAPTER 17
**BLOW YOUR OWN HORN:
COLD-EMAIL OUTREACH** — 97

CHAPTER 18
**MAKING REAL CONNECTIONS—
NETWORKING IS A BAD WORD** — 111

CHAPTER 19
**FINDING FUEL (PART I):
FUNDRAISING FUNDAMENTALS** — 115

CHAPTER 20
**FINDING FUEL (PART II):
VULNERABILITY IS THE KEY** — 121

CHAPTER 21
**FULL STEAM AHEAD!: PRODUCTION** — 125

CHAPTER 22
**JUST KEEP THE WHEELS TURNING:
SELF-DOUBT AND CONFLICT** — 133

## PART III: THE RIDE NEVER ENDS

CHAPTER 23
**MAKING THE MOVIE
IS JUST THE FIRST STOP**     **139**

CHAPTER 24
**GETTING TO THE RIGHT STATIONS:
FESTIVALS**     **147**

CHAPTER 25
**SURROUND YOURSELF
WITH OTHER TRAINS**     **157**

CHAPTER 26
**EVEN WRONG TURNS
CAN MOVE YOU FORWARD**     **161**

CHAPTER 27
**ENJOY THE RIDE**     **165**

| | |
|---|---|
| **RESOURCES** | **169** |
| **OUTLINE** | **193** |
| **BUDGET** | **199** |
| **SCHEDULE** | **203** |
| **INVESTOR DECK** | **207** |
| **ABOUT THE AUTHOR** | **217** |

INTRODUCTION

# HOW I BECAME THE TRAIN

When I first moved to LA, I did everything "by the book." I wanted to be an actress, so I went to casting calls, attended networking events, handed out my card, and waited. "When it's your turn, the right train will come. One call or one email can change everything. Just be patient." That's what people say, right? So I waited for things to happen, for someone to call, for my life to begin.

I'd been told I needed to be "discovered," but that required an agent. To get an agent, I needed to meet one who believed in me. But to meet one who believed in me, I needed to have some impressive work under my belt. To get that work, I needed to be submitted for projects—but, of course, only an agent could do that.

I was stuck in a loop and going nowhere. The reason was simple: I wasn't really *in motion*.

Eventually I got so tired of waiting—waiting for permission, for gatekeepers to let me in, or for someone's email or call to "change my life"—that I reframed everything.

I decided I didn't want to wait at the station anymore. I didn't want to wait for anyone or anything to tell me when to go, what to do, or who to be. I needed to *be* the train. I had to be the one moving forward, letting people jump on board if they wanted to join my journey. By staying in motion, I found a new kind of excitement and energy for my life. I didn't always know exactly where I was headed, but I was in control—and that feeling alone was worth everything.

Being the train doesn't mean there won't be bumps in the road. It means taking charge of the energy with which you move forward. By moving, you create momentum, and that momentum can accomplish more for you than anything or anyone else can. Nobody can support you as fully as you can support yourself. No one will believe in you more than you, and no one will bet on you unless you are willing to bet on yourself. And really, what is life about if not placing that bet on your dreams and your ability to bring them to life?

Someone once asked me, "Why did you choose to think of yourself as a train?" Maybe I subconsciously drew inspiration from *The Little Engine That Could*, but consciously, I knew that I couldn't rely on any one thing or one person to drive my career forward. I needed to be that passionate, powerful, unstoppable machine—one that would inspire others to join in my vision.

Creating three feature films, a comedy special, and a career based on making things happen for myself inspired me to write this book. Part of me thought I should wait until I was famous to write it—but that's completely against what I'm preaching here, which is to *stop waiting for the train to arrive*. Be the train. And since I made that decision, which was after a year of waiting around for things to happen in Los Angeles, that's how I've approached everything in my life.

To be the train means to take control of your journey as a filmmaker, embracing momentum, resilience, and the courage to act.

Rather than waiting for the "perfect" moment or opportunity, being the train is about building your own path forward, adapting to challenges, and seizing chances as they come. It's about moving with intention, ready to pivot when obstacles arise, and being willing to knock on every door—or follow up as many times as it takes—to push your project to the next stage. Whether it's self-distributing your film, cold emailing industry leaders, or forming partnerships, being the train means refusing to let setbacks halt your progress. By building your own momentum and inspiring others to join the journey, you drive your career forward with purpose and authenticity.

For a year, I tried to raise a million dollars for a film. And I kept running into these two infuriating questions: "What's the last thing you've done? And how much money did it make?"

How was I supposed to have a last project if no one would give me the money to make my first project? It was frustrating, to say the least. Here I was, with a master's degree from the American Film Institute (the top film school in the world), a solid script, and a short (*Real Love*) that had done well on the festival circuit and won awards—all the things they tell you that you need—and yet, no one wanted to give me a million dollars. Not even close.

I felt stuck again. So, I started thinking about what I could do to prove that I had what it took to make a feature film. And then it hit me: The only way to prove I could make a feature was to make a feature. But how, when no one was giving me any money?

That's when I realized I didn't need a million dollars. What I did need was a script that could be made on a very low budget. I took a deep dive into my own life and thought about what resources I had access to. And at that moment, I realized something important: I didn't want to wait any longer for the train to arrive. It wasn't coming. I had to *be* the train to make things happen. So, that's exactly what I did.

I told Dan, my husband (who's also my business partner and the director of all the films I've written, produced, and starred in), that we needed to set a date, and we would be filming on that date no matter what. Luckily, I married someone just as crazy as I am (maybe more so!). He said, "Let's do it." So, I started writing a script based on everything I could get for free—there's a whole chapter on this—and we set a shoot date: November 15. It was six months from when we decided to make a movie to when we said we were going to shoot it. And guess what? We stuck to it. High stakes? You bet. But that's how I like it.

You're either all in or you're out.

It wasn't easy, and I'll get into the details later. But we were filming by November 15, and it took a huge amount of work. We even raised more money than I expected by the time we shot it. The key was this: The moment I was sure it was happening, everyone else started to believe it too. People gave us money, and we made the movie. I wrote the outline in a month and the first draft of that script in a few days. We obviously had various drafts that came after, but once we had the first draft, we were already in motion getting all the other moving pieces together.

That was in 2016. Since then, we've made three feature films, a comedy special, a digital series, and a lot of other projects for other people. Our first feature, *The Best People*, was sold to Samuel

Goldwyn Films (MGM) and distributed to over forty countries. Our second feature, *Single Mother by Choice*, was sold directly to HBO, and we doubled our investment. My stand-up comedy special, *2 Moms 1 Mic* (with Kaela Crawford), is on Amazon Prime, as is my digital series, *Tuning In*. Our third feature, *You, Me & Her*, has a 100 percent score on Rotten Tomatoes and has won fourteen awards. For that project, we have formed a first-of-its-kind partnership for its national theatrical run that—if all goes well—could disrupt the entire film industry by using cutting-edge technology to connect filmmakers and producers directly with theater owners.

I've also been hired to write screenplays for other creators, and some of my scripts are currently being packaged at higher budgets. Oh, and I've done all of this without an agent. People are always shocked when they find that out. People in the film industry have been conditioned to think we need an agent to do anything, but I'm proof that's not true. After our first feature, we did get a fantastic manager, Doug Warner, and we are eternally grateful for him. But I had to be the engine that got everything moving, and I still am.

I feel compelled to write this book to share how I've done it—not just the logistics but also the mindset that has made it all possible. You can make the project of your dreams happen without relying on anyone else to open the doors for you.

People keep calling me for advice on how to make their first feature, and I realized—why not write it all down? My way isn't the only way, but it's worked for me, and I want to help others get started too.

Each chapter of this book is going to be short but packed with real advice on how to start your train, stay on track, and finish the journey. Along the way, you'll learn how to be persistent, thoughtful, and strategic. I can't promise you that everything you want will happen, but I can promise that if you follow these guidelines, you'll end up with something valuable that could launch your career. Whether you went to film school or not, making your first feature is a learning process—and in many ways, it's a film school of its own.

Making movies isn't easy. But there's nothing like seeing an idea grow from thin air into a finished product that people can watch, relate to, and hopefully enjoy. And even if they hate it, there's a weird kind of pleasure in knowing you made something that sparked strong feelings in others.

Anyway, let's get started—because there's no better time than now.

PART I

# ALL ABOARD!

CHAPTER 1

# WRITE YOUR OWN YOUR TICKET

Starting is always the hardest part. Even writing this book was hard to start. Why? Because starting means you're putting yourself out there, and that makes you vulnerable. It's a lot scarier to say, "I'm writing a book" or "I'm making a movie" than it is to say, "I'm watching TV tonight." The stakes feel higher when you're stepping into a creative space. There's more to lose when you pursue something big, something that matters to you. Failure suddenly becomes a possibility, and for some reason, we've created this massive resistance to the idea of failure. (I personally love failure, and I'll explain why later.)

The moment you tell someone your goal, the stakes rise even more. Now you feel like you owe it to them to follow through. Personally, my word means a lot to me. If I say I'm going to do something, I want to make sure I do it. But life is full of complications—so much of it is out of our control. The only thing we can control is how we move forward. That's why I'm urging you: *If you've wanted to make a movie your whole life* (whether you are nineteen or seventy-five, it doesn't matter—years are years of wanting something), *start now.*

Tell people you're making your first movie. Let them hold you accountable. You know how people tell you when they're on a diet? They make sure you know that they're serious and that they won't be indulging for a while. It's the same thing here. When I started my master's program at AFI, one of the mentors told us to call our families and give them a heads-up: "I'm going to be MIA for a while." At first, I thought, *That's a pretty intense phone call to make.* But they were right. Telling the people around us gave them time to process it and adjust their expectations of our availability. It was necessary.

So today, I invite you to *state it aloud*—even if you have no idea how it's going to happen. Because here's a secret: No one ever knows exactly how it's going to happen. But that's not the point. The point is to start telling people. Start telling yourself. Start believing it. "I'm going to make my first feature." Say it. The simple act of stating your intention out loud starts a chain reaction. Without this first step, there is no second step. And while this might seem small or even silly, trust me; it's a profound and life-changing moment. It's the act of conceptualizing your dream, calling it in, and speaking it into existence so often that soon there's no alternative reality. You've set the train in motion.

As you share your goal, you'll start to find people who are in the same space, who might want to help you, who inspire you with their advice. You'll also run into people who think it's a terrible idea, who will tell you that you can't do it. And you know what? You need those people, too. You need the naysayers. Because without them, are you really making an impact? (Okay, I'm half joking here. We could all live without the haters, but let's be real—they're part of the journey.) People will say you can't do it because doing things is hard. Not doing things is easy. And most people? They stick with easy.

But you're not most people. That's why you're here. That's why you picked up this book. You're ready to get started, and you're not waiting for anyone's permission. No one can stop you.

CHAPTER 2

# BE THE TRAIN

People will tell you a lot of things—things designed to make you doubt yourself, shrink your dreams, or convince you that the "right" way to make a movie involves handing over control to someone else.

- "You're not well known enough as an actor to make a movie happen."
- "No one is going to fund a film with you as the lead."
- "Your script will never sell without a bigger name attached."
- "If you want your movie to get made, you'd better give the directing reins to someone more experienced."

Guess what? Every one of those statements is a lie, dressed up as advice.

### Why You Must Be the Train

Here's something that no one ever tells you: It's just as hard to convince a big-name actor or director to commit to your movie as it is to give yourself permission to star in it. The road to attaching big names is riddled with delays, nos, and cancellations. It's a never-ending maze of *almost, but not quite*.

Imagine this scenario: You somehow secure the funding to get a well-known actor attached to your movie. You go through months of negotiation, excitement, and hope, thinking this is it—the moment everything will come together. Then, a week before production, the actor books a huge studio project that conflicts with your shoot dates. Suddenly, they're gone. You're back to square one, but now it's six months later, and you've burned through a lot of your energy (and maybe some of your money) waiting for something out of your control.

It happens. And it's no one's fault. Everyone's just trying to earn a living, and actors need to prioritize the projects that will propel their careers forward. So, if everything is hard anyway, why not do what you truly want to do?

If you've been dreaming of being the lead actor, director, or screenwriter of your feature, then own that dream. If you let someone else take the reins of your project, you're giving up control of your destination. You're waiting for someone else's train to show up and take you where you want to go. But if you *are* the train, you decide where and when the journey begins. You can start, stop, and change tracks whenever you want. You're the engineer.

### Get Comfortable Being Uncomfortable

Let's be honest: It's going to be uncomfortable. You're taking a bold step, one that requires immense self-belief and resilience. But this discomfort is a sign that you're growing. Think of it this way: A train doesn't start smoothly—it jerks forward, sputters, and struggles to pick up speed. But once it's moving, the momentum is unstoppable.

In filmmaking, the same thing applies. At first, it feels like you're moving in slow motion, second-guessing your decisions, questioning your ability. But if you stick with it, that momentum builds, and suddenly, you're moving at full speed, unstoppable in your pursuit of your vision. Trust the process, even when it's bumpy. It's all part of the ride.

## Own the Track You're On

Even when you are the train, setbacks are inevitable. That's the nature of this journey. But the beauty of being your own train is that you can always get back on track. If one route doesn't work, you can choose another. If one project hits a dead end, you can start a new one. You're not waiting for someone else's train to arrive—you are in charge of your own momentum.

Here's what you need to remember: Everything is hard, but that's why you're here. You wouldn't be reading this book if you didn't love the challenge. And filmmaking, as tough as it is, is where you thrive. So, let the challenges excite you, and let the unknown fuel your creativity.

In the end, this journey isn't just about making your first feature. It's about empowering yourself to take control of your creative path. Be the train that goes wherever it wants to go, and don't wait for anyone to give you permission to get moving.

## Give Yourself the Power

You know what you're capable of better than anyone else. And the truth is, in the beginning, no one is going to be more passionate about your project than you. You can hire the best actors, writers, and directors, but at the end of the day, no one cares about your story the way you do. And that's why you have to be the one to bring it to life.

Being the train will always mean taking on the role of producer, driving everything forward. The producer in you is the force bringing it all to life and making it happen. But that doesn't mean you can't perform other roles as well.

Don't let the industry tell you that you need to fit into their boxes. If you want to be the star of your own movie, be the star. If you want to direct your film, direct it. The only permission you need is your own. The only validation that matters is the one you give yourself.

*Baby Reindeer*, created by Richard Gadd, is a powerful example of an artist being the train and taking full control of their own narrative. Rather than waiting for the "perfect role" or "ideal opportunity," Gadd transformed his personal experiences of being a struggling comedian stalked by a mentally ill woman into a compelling, intimate one-man stage show. By both writing and performing in the piece, he demonstrated fearless self-authorship, embracing his roles as writer, producer, and star. This initiative allowed audiences and industry alike to witness his talent, leading to its adaptation as a scripted series which ultimately landed on Netflix and earned him an Emmy.

Reflecting in his acceptance speech on enduring one of the most traumatic experiences of his life and turning it into a story that resonated with audiences across the world, he said:

> Look—ten years ago I was down and out, right. I never, ever thought I'd get my life together. I never, ever thought

I'd be able to rectify myself with what had happened to me and get myself on my feet again. And now here I am, picking up one of the biggest writing awards in television.

I don't mean that to sound arrogant. I mean that as encouragement for anyone who's going through a difficult time right now to persevere. I don't know much about this life. I don't know why we're here—none of that. But I do know that nothing lasts forever. And no matter how bad it gets, it always gets better. So if you're struggling, keep going. Keep going, and I promise you, things will be okay.

If you've been waiting for a sign to take the leap and declare yourself the lead, the director, or the writer of your project, this is it. The only thing stopping you is the story you tell yourself. So, rewrite that story.

Say it one more time:

"I am going to direct my first feature. I am going to star in my first feature. I am going to make this happen."

Believe it. Say it until you feel it in your bones. And then be the train that brings it to life.

CHAPTER 3

# DON'T GET STUCK AT THE STATION

Making a movie is a lot like having a baby. You'll never feel fully prepared, but when it happens, if it's something you truly want, you'll step into the role, and you'll crush it. So, if you want to wait for the perfect moment to make your movie, I won't judge you. But maybe this book isn't for you.

So, now that you've committed to the project—you've said it a few times to yourself, maybe even to your grandma or a neighbor—you're thinking: *What's next?*

Here's what's next. Start by asking yourself three important questions:

1. What do you care about?
2. What do you need to say?
3. What is available to you?

Let's break these down a bit. You can write this down for yourself—no need to share it with anyone yet. But, if you want, you can pick one to three cheerleaders—people who are in your camp and rooting for you. They could be friends, family members, anyone who believes in you and who's fun to bounce ideas off of. Share with them if you like, but don't go too wide with this just yet. Ideas change a lot in the early stages, so wait until you have a shooting script before you tell everyone and their mom what your movie is about.

## What Do You Care About?

This is the first big question, and it's a tough one. But it's important. Write down the things you think about regularly and why you think about them. For me, I think a lot about relationships. I'm fascinated by why people behave the way they do and what our interactions with others reveal about us. I love exploring human flaws, especially when it comes to strong, overachieving women who think they don't need anyone else's help. (Am I talking about myself? Maybe a little! Just kidding. Sort of.)

As you start breaking down what you care about, patterns will emerge. For me, these themes pop up in everything I make—even unintentionally! When you lean into what you care about, you start to develop your voice. Maybe you care deeply about ecology, politics, or family dynamics. Whatever it is, the most important thing is that *you care*, because that passion is what will make your film resonate.

And hey, if your dream is to make a horror sci-fi movie about aliens turning into dogs and invading the planet—go for it! But even in a wild concept like that, grounding the story in something that matters to you will elevate it. Maybe one of those aliens has a sick grandfather, and now the movie is about turning back into an alien to save their grandpa. See? Already a better film.

## What Do You Need to Say?

This one can be tricky because, at first, you might feel like you don't *need* to say anything. But think about it like this: If your film is a huge success, you'll be interviewed a hundred times on podcasts, news stations, TV shows—you name it. What's the one thing you could talk about again and again? The message you feel compelled to share with the world?

If you only got to make *one* movie (don't worry—you'll make more!), what would it be about? What's that one story or idea you want to get out into the world, no matter what?

Don't worry—I've wrestled with these same questions more times than I can count. I've agonized over who I am, what I want to say, and whether I'm on the right path. Honestly, I think about that scene in *Zoolander* all the time, where he stares into the spoon, asking, "Who am I?" It's funny, but it's also so relatable! These big questions can feel overwhelming, but don't stress—I've got you covered, and we'll dive deeper into this later on.

## What Is Available to You?

This is the last big question. What can you access for free? Do you have an aunt who lives in an awesome house in Ohio that she might let you film in? (Yes, you'd need to fly to Ohio, but let's put everything on the table for now—we'll break it down later.) Do you have a friend who owns a camera? Maybe someone with an amazing wardrobe? Is there a cute dog you've always wanted to put in a movie? How about your neighbor's backyard? Maybe you live in an apartment with cool, quirky qualities that would make a great set. Or perhaps you have a cousin who's super sweet and would love to act in your film.

Write down every single thing you can think of that you could use in your movie. These should all be free resources. Don't include things like renting a camera from a professional rental house—that's something anyone can do. This list should be *your* special list of resources. Maybe you'll only come up with one thing, or maybe you'll think of tons of options. And if your list ends up being just "my brain and my heart," that's okay, too! But chances are, you'll have a few more things available to you than you realize.

Once you've answered these three key questions, you're ready. The train is already in motion. It's time for the journey. Now let's get going!

CHAPTER 4

# START THE JOURNEY WITH JOY

I wanted to be an actress my whole life. I used to watch movies and copy every scene, acting them out in my room. *Grease* and *Selena* were my obsessions—I knew every line and every song, and I would act out multiple characters. My parents, however, wished I'd pick a new movie, as they were on the verge of losing it!

Acting brought me pure joy. It was exhilarating to know what was coming next, to embody different characters and immerse myself in their world. That joy was what kept me dreaming and moving forward.

I am Mexican-American and was born in the US but moved to Guadalajara, Mexico, when I was two years old. I was mostly raised there. I remember being nine years old, begging my parents to let me act full time instead of going to school. But they insisted I finish my education first, which I now appreciate as a parent myself.

Eventually, I found a way to dip my toes into acting by getting an agent in Guadalajara. I booked some fun gigs, including a kids' TV show (on videocassette!) where I taught aliens to speak English and some modeling jobs for C&A, which was Mexico's equivalent of GAP. But again, my parents kept school as the priority, and juggling both became too difficult. Looking back, I get it—but at the time, all I wanted to do was act.

When I finally moved to Los Angeles at eighteen, I was determined to be an actress. I dove in headfirst but soon fell into a very *La La Land* routine. I'd drive for hours to auditions, wait for my turn, and get two minutes in a room to prove I was right for the role. In those waiting rooms, I started doubting myself. I saw how much more experience others had, how long they had been at it. And the doubt crept in—*I'm not good enough. I'll never book the role. This is too hard.* And what did I do? I gave up.

But let me tell you—this isn't a lesson about giving up. It's about finding your joy again. It's about being the train and realizing that when you lose sight of your passion, you can't move forward.

## The Road to Rediscovery

I decided that producing might give me more control over outcomes. (Spoiler: It didn't.) I went to film school at Loyola Marymount University (LMU), worked in international distribution for a year, then earned a Master of Producing degree from AFI. I spent seven years as a producer and casting director, working on over a hundred projects. I worked with Issa Rae (*Insecure*), Lee Aronsohn (*Two and a Half Men*), Salvador Paskowitz (*The Age of Adaline*), and Rob Schneider (*Deuce Bigalow: Male Gigolo*), among many more. While I was "successful" in many ways, the acting dream still nagged at me. I wasn't enjoying the ride.

One day, I hit an emotional wall. I was working nonstop but hadn't achieved the success markers I had set in my mind—no big film festivals, no feature film of my own, and worst of all, I wasn't even pursuing what I truly loved: acting. Everything felt serious and heavy, and I was burned-out.

Then something clicked: I wasn't having fun anymore. I'd forgotten the joy that had once fueled my creativity. So, I made a shift. I joined the improv group at The Groundlings, enrolled in acting classes at Lesly Kahn, and even took a stand-up comedy class with Lesley Wolff. I told myself that this wasn't about proving anything to anyone—it was about having fun again.

## Creativity in Playfulness

From these classes, everything changed. By having fun and letting myself play, new opportunities started pouring in. During one of my stand-up performances, a booker saw me and invited me to perform at the Comedy Store—one of the biggest comedy venues in Los Angeles. I performed there for almost two years, which led to me cocreating a comedy special with Kaela Crawford—*2 Moms 1 Mic*, now on Amazon Prime and YouTube.

Then, during a performance at the Groundlings, a friend working for the Duplass Brothers saw my monologue and invited me to audition for a digital series they were producing. I hadn't auditioned in ten years, but I booked the part! That moment was a revelation—it was a sign that I was meant to act.

I went on to write, produce, and star in a digital series that was based on that Groundlings monologue (*Tuning In*, which is now also on Amazon Prime and YouTube).

And all of this happened because I found joy in the process again. By not taking myself so seriously and giving myself permission to be playful, I started to move forward. This is what I want to emphasize: Fun fuels creativity. If you want to be the train, you need to enjoy the ride; the journey is long, and you're going to need that fuel.

Not every moment will be fun, but fun is essential to keeping your creative engine running. Whether you want to act, write, direct, or all three, embracing joy will help you reach your destination.

CHAPTER 5

# PLAN YOUR ROUTE: WRITING

For first-time writers, bringing a story to life can be an exhilarating and daunting process.

Writing is both the easiest and hardest step towards being the train. As a writer, you hold immense power. You create the entire story from your brain onto the page, which is an incredible feat!

Without the script, there is no film—unless you're making a documentary, and even then, sometimes a loose script can help. So, let's discuss how to get started and, more importantly, how to write something you can actually bring to life.

**Writing What You Know**
One of the best ways to write something strong and grounded is to draw from what you know. This doesn't mean your story can't be creative or imaginative. It means that the relationships, emotions, and truths you write should come from a place of personal knowledge. For example, if you know your mother's voice so well that you can write her dialogue without ever speaking to her, that's a

great relationship to explore in your writing. Authenticity resonates with audiences, and the more you lean into what feels true to you, the more your film will connect with others.

Low-budget films often succeed when they focus on relationships—dramas, family dynamics, or even character-driven comedies. These stories don't rely on expensive visual effects or massive set pieces but instead on truth, vulnerability, and strong performances. Horror films can also be highly effective on a small budget. Look at *The Blair Witch Project*. Its success came from the rawness and believability of its concept—this is the kind of "realness" that draws audiences in.

Here are some questions to help you start writing:

- What story matters to me enough to commit to writing it as a feature?
- What personal experiences or relationships can I draw from?
- How can I ground the story into a lower-budget production so I can make it happen myself?
- How many characters do I truly need to tell this story?
- What locations do I already have access to (for example, your mom's backyard or your friend's kitchen)?
- When this movie is successful and I'm talking about it every day in interviews, will I still feel passionate and proud of the story I'm sharing?

## Scheduling Your Writing Time

One of the most important aspects of writing a screenplay is discipline. If you don't set a writing schedule, you'll never finish your script.

I like to begin with an outline. I usually spend one to two months on it, writing every day, five days a week. For each writing session, I dedicate thirty minutes to an hour to thinking about the story, followed by two to three hours of actual writing. Writing can be exhausting—mentally and emotionally—and sometimes it feels like you're getting nowhere. But here's the trick: Even on days when you feel blocked or unsure of what to write, stick to your schedule.

Not everyone has endless hours to dedicate to writing, so it's essential to find a structure that suits your lifestyle. How many hours per day or weekends can you realistically devote to writing? When are you most productive? For example, my husband thrives at 4:00 a.m., waking in the middle of the night to write, while I'm most effective around 9:00 a.m. Finding a groove that aligns with your lifestyle is the most crucial step. Start by taking a week to observe your habits and schedule, then craft a writing schedule that aligns with your productivity peaks, availability, and personal rhythm.

Once you've done this, decide how many hours you'll dedicate to writing each day, keeping in mind that it's perfectly fine to skip a day or two as long as you maintain overall consistency. If your initial schedule doesn't work, adjust it—there's no need to feel guilty for not sticking to a rigid plan. The goal is to establish a routine that allows you to find your creative flow, making it easier to enter a productive state. Over time, this practice will become a natural and essential part of your daily life, one you can consistently rely on.

And don't be afraid to write the "bad version." The bad version is essentially a brain dump—messy, too on the nose, and full of ideas that don't quite connect. But without it, you'll never get to the great version. You can't shape a masterpiece if you don't give yourself the freedom to create a rough, imperfect first draft.

At the back of this book, you'll find an early and very rough outline of my movie *Single Mother by Choice*, which was originally titled *37 Weeks*. If you compare this outline to the finished film on HBO Max, you'll notice how much the story evolved, especially after the pandemic forced us to rewrite the script. Interestingly, despite the significant changes, the character's arc and the story's core intention remained intact. This shows that while I had to completely reimagine how to tell the story, my clarity about its message endured.

It also illustrates how to approach creating an outline: it can start rough, serving as a foundation to build on. But over time, you refine it by adding details and depth before transitioning to full-fledged scriptwriting.

### Don't Get Discouraged

For first-time writers, bringing a story to life can be an exhilarating and daunting process. Even if you get beyond the fear of writing the "bad version," writing can be immensely challenging and lonely at times.

The creative process can often feel both challenging and isolating. One of the main reasons for this loneliness is the frustration that arises when you hit a roadblock—whether it's being stuck on a specific story plot or grappling with an unresolved issue in your narrative. Sitting alone in a room, trying to uncover the best path forward, can become overwhelming. The sheer number of possible directions your story can take might paralyze decision-making, making the process feel daunting and draining.

Overcoming creative roadblocks in screenwriting requires a combination of patience, fresh perspective, and structured problem-solving. When stuck, step away from the project to clear your mind—go for a walk, watch a movie, or do something unrelated to writing. Revisiting the story with a fresh perspective can often spark new ideas. Try brainstorming alternative plotlines or character motivations without judgment, focusing on possibilities rather than limitations. Sharing your draft with a trusted collaborator for feedback can also reveal solutions you might not have considered. Most importantly, embrace the process as part of creativity.

## Moving from Outline to Screenplay

When do you know it's time to move from the outline to the screenplay? Honestly, it's a gut feeling, but I usually find it after I've revised my outline a few times. By the time I start writing the script, I want to know exactly what each scene is going to be, what the characters' arcs are, and how the journey will unfold. Sometimes, as I'm outlining, I come up with dialogue or specific moments, and I jot those down to insert later. I'll share one of my outlines later in the book to show you what my process looks like.

For my most recent script, *You, Me & Her*, I outlined for three months, and when the outline was ready, I wrote the first version of the script in forty-eight hours. Of course, that wasn't the final version, but I was able to write quickly because my outline was so detailed and thought-out.

## Writing with Your Producer Brain

First off, I encourage creativity above all else. Write what you love! However, I also encourage practicality, especially for your first feature. If you're writing a screenplay that you intend to make yourself, you need to activate your producer brain. This means being mindful of the budget while writing. Ask yourself if certain elements feel too expensive and, if so, how you can achieve the same emotional or narrative effect in a less costly way.

For instance, while it might be fun to write that your main character owns a lion, consider the logistics of actually getting a lion on set. You'll need a trainer and a company to rent the lion from, which is expensive, and there are limits to how long animals can work on set. You also probably won't have the means to include a realistic CGI lion throughout the film. Maybe instead, your character could own a cat—it could communicate the same idea without breaking the bank. But sometimes, the lion is essential, and in those cases, you might need to fight for that element—or, later in production, accept that you'll have to swap it out for the more budget-friendly cat.

You might be wondering, *Should I wait to start this project until I have enough money to make it exactly as I envisioned—like with a lion?* That's a tough question, and the answer depends on your approach. I can share how I handle it, but that doesn't mean it's the only way.

I see myself as an idea factory—I'm constantly generating fresh, exciting concepts. Because of this, I don't view any single project as *the one,* the golden idea, or the most important thing I'll ever create. Sure, I have bigger-budget projects that I know will require more funding to bring to life. But if my current goal is to make a feature film now, I focus on making my story work within a lower budget, empowering myself to get started.

If my story *absolutely* needs a lion and it can't work without it, then maybe I need to explore a different idea. But if I can adapt the lion into something like a cat, and the story still holds up, then I can keep moving forward.

It's also perfectly okay to write something you don't want to make right now. Creativity is like being the train—it's all about staying in motion. However, this book is about helping you achieve a fully funded feature on a shoestring budget, with the flexibility to expand your story if you end up with more resources than you expected.

## Adapting Intellectual Property (IP)

This route is an exciting option, though not without its challenges. IP can be anything you acquire the rights to for a mutually agreed time period—books, podcasts, articles, life rights, and even toys like Barbie!

I once tried to adapt a book called *Amando a Pablo, Odiando a Escobar*, which is about Pablo Escobar's lover. It's an incredible, female-driven story, and I was obsessed with making it into a film. After months of research, I discovered that the author had changed her name for safety reasons, making it impossible to contact her. A few years later, I saw the movie promoted at the Cannes Film Festival, produced by Javier Bardem! I actually met him at a party and asked how he got the rights—turns out, he hired a private investigator to find the author. I'm not Javier Bardem, and I definitely couldn't afford a PI.

Still, I have friends who've successfully acquired rights to books and articles, and it can be a smooth process. It all depends on getting in touch with the rights owner and negotiating a time frame to make the project happen. Keep in mind, though, that when working with IP, creators can be very particular about their property. They might want script approval or involvement as a writer, and budget negotiations can become trickier.

If you're pursuing IP, consider getting a shopping agreement, where you have the rights for a set time period. I'd recommend securing at least two years, as it can take time to get funding, especially for larger-budget projects.

Adapting IP requires patience and creativity. The key is to ensure everyone is aligned with the creative vision. Misalignment between parties can derail the project, as I've experienced. When two creators don't share the same vision, the project can stall indefinitely.

**Taking Over a Stalled Project or Preexisting Script**
Taking over a preexisting project can feel like a relief—you're starting with a script, which saves time! However, it's important to have clear conversations with the writer about your vision for the project.

If you are planning to rewrite the script, make sure to make that clear from the beginning and set expectations. Do you want the writer's input throughout? If so, how much? Do they need to approve changes? Write down what both parties should expect and talk it through in detail. Afterward, create a contract you both agree on. Clear communication ensures that everyone is on the same track, avoiding unnecessary conflicts down the line.

**Making a Stop for Feedback**
Whatever story you're telling, feedback is crucial. You won't always agree with everyone's feedback, and that's okay. But the more perspectives you get, the more you'll start to see patterns in the feedback. If multiple people point out the same issue, it might be worth rethinking.

For my and my husband's first feature, we held a test screening with a questionnaire. Almost no one liked the beginning. It was tough to hear, but it was clear that something wasn't landing, so we reshot the beginning.

Reshooting the beginning of this movie was by far the most crucial decision we made. After seeing how everything came together, it became clear that these adjustments were essential for the entire character arc to work. We had to reimagine what those scenes would look like and figure out how to execute them on a very tight budget. (Pro tip: always budget at least one day for reshoots—it can be a lifesaver in postproduction!) The film improved tremendously after we added the reshot scenes, making the story much stronger overall.

Ask for feedback when you're near the end of the edit but still have time to make changes. The same goes for the script—when you think you've nailed it, send it to ten people and see what they say. If something comes up more than once, reconsider that element.

## Keep Pushing Forward

There are many ways to create your story route, whether you're adapting existing IP, taking over a stalled project, or building a story from scratch. The key is knowing what excites you, embracing collaboration, and being open to feedback.

Writing a screenplay to make yourself is a lot more work than writing a screenplay to sell. But if you're committed to being the train and driving this project forward, it's worth the effort.

If your goal is just to sell the script, that's totally valid too—just know that it requires patience. I prefer not to wait for anyone, which is why I'm my own train on every project.

Writing is your first step in making your movie real. Keep pushing forward, and you'll find the path that works for you.

Be intentional, be practical, and most importantly—be the train!

CHAPTER 6

# EVERYONE YOU KNOW IS A POTENTIAL PASSENGER: CHARACTERS

Now for my favorite part of making every movie: creating the characters!

When crafting your characters, consider how to bring them to life in a realistic way. Think of every film you've ever loved and reflect on the main character—what made them likable or unlikable? What kept you engaged as they went on their journey?

I've read many screenplays with characters who sound like stereotypes or where you could swap any character for another without consequence. This is what I would call a bad script—an uninteresting screenplay. Specificity is essential for your characters to jump off the page. What makes people specific?

Think about the people you already know. Everyone in your life—your quirky friends, family, and colleagues—can inspire dynamic, relatable characters. By observing these individuals and using them as a foundation, you can create characters who feel genuine and compelling, helping to drive your story forward.

For example, my first feature, *The Best People* (available to watch on Tubi and Amazon Prime) is about two sisters—something I could easily relate to since I'm one of two sisters. At that point in my career, I hadn't yet decided to return to acting because I was living in fear of not being good enough. So, I wrote the script with a good friend in mind. She's insanely talented, and I believed she'd be perfect as the lead actress.

When I say I wrote with her in mind, I'm referring to how the character speaks—the tone, the phrases, the way she expresses herself—though the character itself was loosely based on my own life experiences. I think I may have made my friend a little uncomfortable when I presented the script to her because it sounded so much like her, even though the character was not her at all, but I also believe she was flattered. It was a huge compliment. I wanted her to star in it, and she did.

Another example—I have a family member who is incredibly negative but always manages to say negative things with a smile on their face. It's strangely endearing, and I've always wanted to write a character like this. Then there's someone who feels the need to fill their water cup even when it's completely full. This peculiar behavior hints at deeper issues but offers an interesting attribute to observe—no matter how full the glass is, they must top it off.

You can find these attributes in every interaction you have and every decision you make. Character is about what people wear, how they talk, and why they do what they do. Sometimes I even observe a stranger doing something bizarre and write it down—a practice I learned at the Groundlings.

Noticing these kinds of behaviors in people is what gives characters their authenticity. The more authentic and realistic your characters seem, the more likely it is that audiences will relate to them and, consequently, to your film.

It's crucial to remember that you can't just write about someone without their permission. However, you can take pieces of different people's attributes and create a unique character that has never been seen before.

Once you have a character in mind, consider these thought-provoking questions:

1. What is their biggest inner desire?
2. What do they say they care about, and what do they actually care about?
3. What do they lie about?
4. What keeps them up at night?
5. What's funny about them?
6. Is there any physical habit that reveals something about who they are?
7. What do they love or hate about themselves?
8. What is their blind spot?
9. What are they willing to do to get what they want?
10. Do they know what they want?
11. What makes them unique?
12. How do their culture and upbringing affect their day-to-day behavior?

These questions can help you build upon the characters you've already written, adding more specificity and depth.

To me, characters are everything, especially in low-budget filmmaking. No matter what genre you're in, if your main character can get hit by a bus and no one cares, you've failed. People need to invest in the characters to watch the movie and discuss it afterward. So, take the time to really consider who you want to write about and why. The more real these characters feel, and the more compelling your reasons for writing about them, the better your chances of making a successful movie.

CHAPTER 7

# ASK EVERYONE TO JUMP IN: YOUR AUDIENCE WANTS TO RIDE WITH YOU

If you're already a content creator with a following, congratulations! You're light-years ahead of most filmmakers, who often spend their entire careers trying to crack the code on understanding their audiences.

You already know who you're speaking to, what they respond to, and what makes them want to come back for more. That's a huge accomplishment in itself! The rest should be smooth sailing, right? Just kidding! Creating from here isn't easy either, but you've tackled one of the biggest hurdles.

A while back, Dan and I had the opportunity to work with a very popular Instagram influencer, writing a feature with his online persona as the central character. We loved his content, and working side by side to build a story around his brand was a blast. The film was a musical comedy—a fun, new genre for us—and when the script was ready, we had a great plan to raise funds directly from his fan base. His followers were already invested in his content, so why not invite them to be part of this project? But then there was a big market crash. The influencer decided crowdfunding wasn't the right move during such a time, so the project went on hold.

I still hope we can revive it someday; I'm a huge fan of his, and the script deserves its moment. Even though it ultimately didn't work out, that experience drove home the great potential of crowdsourcing as a way to build all-important momentum (as well as a lesson in not stalling for too long—keep the wheels turning!).

For those of you with an engaged audience, you should absolutely consider creating a feature around your characters or brand. Your audience already loves you and wants to see more, so give them that!

Another amazing aspect of having a fan base is the built-in creative community. You can crowdsource ideas, ask for feedback, and make them part of the whole journey. People love getting an inside look at the creative process, even if they're not filmmakers. Everybody has an opinion about what works and what doesn't, and people will feel that much more invested if they get to help shape your story. Giving your audience that insider access is huge!

Even if you don't have a large following on social media, it's still essential to engage in crowdsourcing and building a sense of community by sharing your journey along the way. Creating a *fan base* is one of the most powerful ways to accelerate your career. While you may not have a significant number of supporters at the start, consistency in sharing content and involving others in your creative process will naturally increase engagement among those who do care. As these connections deepen, word of mouth will help your audience grow organically. Remember, everyone starts somewhere. Empower yourself by inviting others to be part of your creativity—share your vision, your progress, and your passion. As you do, you'll see your fan base and your opportunities expand.

So, if you're thinking of making a film, start by choosing a story that speaks directly to your audience. They're already on this ride with you, cheering you on, so create something that will keep them on board. You know what they want, and you know how to deliver it with your signature style. Make them feel like VIPs on this ride by involving them from the start. Share your vision, take polls, ask questions, and let them in on the creative highs and lows. You're already good at crafting stories they love, so this is just another way to deepen that connection.

Here are some tips to get you rolling:

- **Take inventory of what you already have.** Use the resources around you and lean into your strengths. Already have character ideas? Perfect. Built-in settings you know? Even better. Your fans will enjoy a familiar environment brought to life. And don't worry about fancy equipment. Sean Baker shot *Tangerine* on an iPhone, won the Sundance Film Festival, and launched his career to new heights. If he can do it, so can you! Okay, we have to acknowledge he's a genius. But hey, who said you're not?
- **Use feedback from your community.** Involve your fans in early brainstorming sessions or poll them on story arcs they'd be excited to see. It's like getting live market research while building hype.
- **Consider small crowdfunding or subscription models.** If you're ready to start production, look at crowdfunding from your followers or launching a subscription-based model where fans get exclusive updates. This can help fund the film while keeping fans engaged.

- **Share progress through behind-the-scenes content.** Show the production's journey—behind-the-scenes moments, day-to-day updates, and challenges you're facing. People love feeling like they're part of something big.
- **Focus on one key theme.** Select a theme that resonates deeply with you and with your followers. If your usual content revolves around humor, lifestyle, or personal growth, pick a storyline that plays to that strength, making the experience familiar yet fresh.

Ultimately, your job here is to create an experience for everyone on board. This is an authentic, collaborative journey with the people who have been riding along with you from the start. So, keep doing what you're already great at, share the magic, and let your fans be part of creating something bigger than just the next video. This time, you're giving them a feature film. And trust me—they'll be thrilled to be part of that journey with you.

CHAPTER 8

# BE THE ENGINE: PRODUCING

Producing a movie—or anything in life—comes down to resourcefulness. And you, my friend, are clearly resourceful! You've bought this book because you're serious about making your film, and now you're breaking down the steps to get there. That's a great start.

I often joke that being a producer is like being everyone's mother, assistant, therapist, and CEO all at once. You're the person everyone looks to when there's a problem to solve, but you're also the one leading the charge, keeping things moving forward, and ensuring that the vision for the film is realized.

## The Different Types of Producers

It's common to feel confused by the sheer number of producers in a film's credits. Each type of producer has a specific role, and it's important to understand them so you can figure out which role you're best suited for (and which roles you might need to fill as you build your team).

- **Producer (you):** This is the main producer who oversees everything—creative, budget, schedule, crew, story development, and talent casting. You'll wear many hats in this role, taking a 360-degree view of the project from preproduction to postproduction, marketing, and distribution. It's essential for anyone making their own projects happen to take on the role of this type of proactive producer. No one will care about your story as deeply as you do, which means you need to ensure the project keeps moving forward at every step. Regardless of any other roles you may want to take on, it's your responsibility to champion your story and push it toward completion.
- **Executive producer:** This is usually the person who brings in the money or talent. They're often not involved in the day-to-day production, but they play a crucial role in securing funding or high-profile actors.
- **Line producer:** This person focuses on the budget and schedule. They help with hiring the crew and making sure everything runs smoothly within the constraints of time and money. More on this in Part II.
- **Associate producer:** This title can mean a few different things—it could be someone who helped with story notes, a friend who worked on set for free, or someone who made a crucial phone call to secure a key resource. You might be thinking to yourself, *Okay, Selina, I get that you can do all sorts of random tasks and still be credited as an associate producer—but what's the actual definition of the job?* If you look it up, you'll find the role is incredibly broad and varies widely. That's

exactly why I'm being upfront about the real reason people receive this credit—it's flexible and depends on the specific circumstances of a project.

- **Assistant producer:** This person works as the producer's assistant, helping with whatever is needed, from coordinating schedules to handling logistics.
- **Production coordinator/coordinating producer:** This person handles logistics, problem-solving, and a million phone calls about things like parking, permits, and other production details. They work closely with the line producer and unit production manager (UPM). The UPM works with the line producer and ensures that the project runs smoothly, stays on schedule, and remains within budget.

There are more types of producers, but for the purposes of your indie feature, these roles are the key players.

### How to Be a Great Producer

If you are organized, love problem-solving, and can manage different personalities, producing is probably the job for you. It's not glamorous, but it's one of the most essential roles in filmmaking. A great producer keeps the train running smoothly, ensuring that every department has what it needs while staying on budget and on schedule.

Here are a few key tips for producing your first feature:

1. **Start with a realistic budget.** Be clear about what your budget can cover and where you'll need to cut corners.

Creativity will come into play when you're faced with financial limitations.
2. **Build a reliable crew.** Surround yourself with people who are talented, dedicated, and willing to go the extra mile for the project. Sometimes passion is more valuable than experience.
3. **Keep everyone motivated.** Morale can dip during production—long hours, tight schedules, and unforeseen challenges can take a toll. Your role is to keep the team motivated and focused on the goal. One of the most important skills you'll need is the ability to maintain a positive attitude.
4. **Be a problem solver.** No matter how well you plan, something will go wrong. It's your job to stay calm, think creatively, and find solutions quickly. Even if you don't have all the answers, your resourcefulness and positive energy will carry the project forward.

Producing is a balancing act of logistics, creativity, and people management. But, as daunting as it might seem, it's also incredibly rewarding to see all your hard work come together on-screen.

## Leveraging Your Community and Resources

Tapping into your connections is key. You'll need to build a good crew, find talented actors, and secure resources for your production—sometimes on a shoestring budget. This is where your community comes into play. Think about grants for low-budget filmmakers, in-kind donations from equipment companies, or food donations from local businesses. Depending on your film's subject matter, you can even find companies willing to sponsor certain aspects of the production.

Asking for favors is part of the indie filmmaker's tool kit. Don't be afraid to reach out to your friends, family, and professional contacts. People want to help, especially if they believe in your vision. Producing is about being persistent and unafraid to ask for what you need.

Think outside the box and be resourceful with your team. For example, I've collaborated with talented students from the Fashion Institute of Design & Merchandising as costume designers. While they weren't formally trained for this specific role, their skills in fashion and design translated beautifully into creating costumes for an independent short film. Early in your career, it's essential to partner with passionate, like-minded individuals eager to learn and grow. Often, people excel in roles outside their formal training when given the opportunity to explore and contribute creatively.

Also—ask people what they're good at! When I first started, I had friends join my crews, and I would simply ask about their strengths, then assign them roles accordingly. While not everyone on your team needs to lack experience—especially for critical positions where expertise can streamline production—some roles, like production assistant or production coordinator, benefit more from traits like organization, hard work, and attention to detail. That person could even be your sister or best friend. This approach opens up creative ways to assemble your team and get started.

So, if you're taking on the challenge of being the engine of your own film, buckle up! Producing is an exciting, exhausting, and ultimately empowering role that puts you in control of bringing your vision to life.

CHAPTER 9

# BE THE ENGINEER: DIRECTING

For first-time directors, stepping into the director's chair might feel like an enormous leap. You are at the controls, steering the entire production toward your creative vision, even if you've never directed before.

Directing a feature means you're overseeing everything, from the conception of the story to the final sound mix. You're responsible for bringing it all together in a cohesive, creative way. This means not just focusing on the individual pieces—story, performance, production design, cinematography, editing, and music—but understanding how they all interact. It's essential to maintain a strong vision throughout the entire process, from the earliest stages of development to the final cut. You must have a unified idea of what you want the film to be, and you need to communicate that to every department.

## How to Lead Without Prior Experience

If this is your first time directing, you might feel some imposter syndrome. After all, everyone on set will be looking to you for guidance, and you've never done this before. It's okay to not have all the answers—no first-time director does. What's more important is your ability to communicate your vision, steer the team, and keep everyone aligned with your creative goals.

Here are some tips for managing the crew as a first-time director:

- **Be confident in your vision.** Even if you don't have technical expertise in every department, you need to have a strong sense of what you want. Your confidence will inspire others to trust your direction.
- **Learn from your team.** You'll likely have crew members with more experience than you in certain areas, like cinematography or production design. Be open to their suggestions while staying true to your vision.
- **Be kind but assertive.** Directors who lead with respect and clear communication often get the best out of their team. Know when to listen and when to push back (respectfully) if something doesn't align with your overall vision.
- **Do the prep work.** Preparation is key to a smooth production. Familiarize yourself with the script, shot lists, and schedules and ensure that everyone on your team is on the same page before filming begins.

## How to Handle Mistakes

One of the hardest things for a first-time director to accept is that mistakes are part of the process. Filmmaking is messy, and things rarely go exactly as planned. Budgets get slashed, actors get sick, locations fall through, and shots don't turn out the way you imagined.

What separates successful directors from others is their ability to adapt and course-correct. Being able to shift gears when something goes offtrack is crucial. This doesn't mean compromising your vision but finding creative ways to navigate around the obstacles that will inevitably arise.

For example, during one shoot, an actor unexpectedly fell ill and couldn't make it on the day we had booked a location specifically for their scene. We were already on set when we found out, and the situation was urgent. My husband took a moment to assess the options and decided to rewrite the scene on the spot. He adjusted it so the actor wasn't necessary, yet the character's arc still progressed. It was a tough call, but since our budget didn't allow for a reshoot, this solution worked—and it ultimately fit well in the final cut.

## How to Position Yourself as a Director

Being a first-time feature director is an enormous responsibility. You're not only directing the movie; you're also convincing people—whether they are investors, producers, or actors—that you're the right person for the job despite your lack of experience. Here's how you can position yourself as a director and confidently take the reins of your first feature film:

1. **Write your own ticket.** If you wrote the script, you're already one step ahead. As the writer, you can tell potential collaborators that this is your story and you're going to direct it. It's a bold statement, but it's one that's necessary if you want to be in control of your vision. At some point, you have to make it clear:

*I will direct this feature.* No one is going to give you permission—you have to take it.

2. **Find the right script and connect with it.** If you're not a writer or haven't written your own material, finding the right script is crucial. You need to connect deeply with the story you're telling. Why are *you* the right person to direct this film? This connection is more important than technical knowledge—directing a film is about having an undeniable bond with the material. If you didn't write the script, take the time to find or develop a relationship with a writer who can help you find that story.

3. **Develop a visual deck.** A visual deck is a powerful tool to communicate your vision to potential collaborators. Once you have your script, create a visual deck that includes the following:

    - **The story:** Write a clear summary of the plot and themes.
    - **The director's statement:** Explains why this story is important, both to you and to your audience. This might include explaining your personal connection to the material and (implicitly or explicitly) why you're the best person to direct it.
    - **Visual references:** Provide collages of images, colors, and tones that represent the look and feel of the film.
    - **Your bio:** Include your background, experience, and other reasons why you're qualified to direct.

- **Your team:** If you've already started building a crew, include their bios as well.

This deck will show potential investors, producers, and collaborators that you have a clear vision and the passion to execute it.

4. **Build your team.** As a director, you need a strong team around you. If you're not highly experienced, working with people who are can help balance the load, but beware of bringing on people with *too* much experience. They might see you as a novice and bring a sense of superiority to the set, which can be challenging to navigate. Start by building relationships with people who believe in you and your vision. Reach out to film schools, attend festivals, or ask for recommendations from peers. Find a cinematographer, production designer, and editor who are excited about the project and are willing to work with you, even if it's on a lower budget. It's important to work with people you trust and can communicate with openly.

You can find talented crew members in a variety of places, including local film schools. Posting on a school's job board, reaching out to instructors, or emailing the program director can be very effective. I've often contacted directors from schools like Fashion Institute of Design & Merchandising (for costume designers) or LMU, American Film Institute (AFI), University of California—LA (UCLA), University of Southern California (USC), and New York

Film Academy (NYFA) for various production roles, and many of my hires have come from these programs.

In addition to film schools, be sure to check the resources at the back of this book for a comprehensive list. There are numerous online platforms where you can post job listings, such as the Mandy Network, ProductionHUB, and Stage 32. You can also look into industry-focused Facebook groups, film commission websites, and local arts organizations that connect filmmakers with crew members. Communities like Film Independent, NALIP, and Women in Film are also great resources for finding crew members. Events, mixers, and even LinkedIn can help you build your production team. By exploring a wide range of options, you'll increase your chances of finding the right crew for your project.

### How to Be the Creative Force

Directing is a creative marathon. It's not about having all the technical skills but about problem-solving and making decisions that protect your vision. Dan, who has directed several features, always has the entire team watch the same reference films, which are tailored to the tone and style he's trying to create, before production starts. This helps the crew understand the visual aesthetic he's aiming for. Even if budget constraints arise, creativity can allow you to achieve your vision in unexpected ways.

Remember, you are the driving force behind this project. You set the tone, you steer the train, and everyone will look to you for guidance. It's not an easy job, but it's incredibly rewarding. Keep your vision clear, communicate with your team, and learn to adapt when things go offtrack. If you can do that, you're ready to be the engineer of your first feature film.

By positioning yourself confidently, connecting deeply with the material, and being the captain of your creative ship, you can step into the role of director with purpose and vision. Mistakes will happen, but that's part of the journey. Be bold, be decisive, and most importantly, be the train.

CHAPTER 10

# BE THE LEAD CAR: STARRING

Whether you've just started acting or have been doing it for years, there's one truth I've learned: Some roles are amazing, and some, well, suck. The difference comes down to how well written the roles are.

The awesome ones feel specific, are three-dimensional, and allow you to fully immerse yourself in the character. On the other hand, the roles that fall flat feel generic, like they could be played by anyone, and sometimes, they don't even make sense within the story.

Here's what I know from my experience as a writer: Even those seemingly insignificant, less-specific roles are still important. They deserve your full effort because you never know when a small part might turn into something bigger. As a casting director, whenever I saw an actor truly shine in a role—no matter how small—I'd bring them back again and again. And even if they didn't land the part, the directors and I would always remember them because they stood out. Often, casting decisions come down to something as simple as the director's vision rather than an actor's talent. But if you nail a performance, people will remember you. Trust me; that impression lasts.

Now, let's talk about a challenge that might feel familiar: waiting for that perfect role to come along. For many actors, it can take years to land a role that feels worthy of their talent. This isn't because they aren't good enough; it's because the competition is fierce, and many directors prefer to work with actors they already trust. It's a tough business, and while some directors are open to taking risks on fresh faces, it can be incredibly frustrating to constantly feel like you're waiting for your shot.

So, here's what I did to take control: I started writing my own roles. You might be thinking, *I'm not a writer* or *I've done this before, but I don't have the money to produce it.* Don't worry—we'll cover the financing and logistics later in the book. For now, let's focus on why writing a role for yourself is one of the most empowering things you can do. As actors, we are all observers of human behavior, and that's what writing is too—capturing and interpreting behavior. Acting is about exploring what makes people tick, and writing is just another extension of that.

You don't have to be the next Aaron Sorkin to write a role for yourself. You just need to create a character that speaks to you—one that allows you to showcase your strengths as an actor. And while this book focuses on a feature film, don't forget that you can start smaller. You can write a short film, a digital series, or anything that feels manageable. The important part is creating a character that feels authentic to you.

When I write for myself, I like to imagine characters that could have been me—iterations of who I might have become if my life had taken a different turn. These characters aren't exactly me, but they share parts of my personality, my flaws, my strengths, and my essence. By making these characters specific to who I am, I create roles that would be difficult for anyone else to play. This ensures that when I star in my own film, it feels genuine, and people watching will think, *Wow, that was so real.*

Let's get you started on crafting a role for yourself. Here are a few writing prompts to guide you:

- **What genre do I love?**

  - What kind of film would I love to act in? Am I drawn to slapstick comedy, romantic dramas, psychological thrillers, or horror? Think about your favorite movie scenes and the types of characters you've always wanted to portray. Identifying your favorite genre will help shape the type of character you create.

- **What are my strengths and flaws as a person?**

  - This is a personal reflection, so no need to share with anyone unless you want to. Ask yourself what you're really good at and where you might struggle. For example, I know that I love being in control, but the truth is, I'm not always as in control as I think I am. That self-awareness led me to create a character who shares this trait—someone who believes they have it all figured out only to discover they don't.

- What are my blind spots?

    - A blind spot is something about yourself over which you don't have much control and perhaps are not fully aware of doing while you're doing it. For me, it's my constant need to be in control (oh, the irony), which often pulls me out of the present moment. Think about how a blind spot could create conflict for your character. How does this flaw affect their daily life, their relationships, and their decisions?

- How can I exaggerate these traits to make my character more compelling?

    - Take a strength or flaw of yours and amplify it. What would happen if your character took this trait to the extreme? For example, when I wrote my character in "I Call the Shots," the first monologue I performed at a Groundlings class, I exaggerated my own tendencies for control and put her in a dating scenario where her need to manage every aspect of the date completely sabotages her chances.

- How can I create a separation from myself while still relating to the character?

    - You don't have to play yourself. Create a character that shares parts of your personality but isn't exactly you. For my character in "I Call the Shots," I drew inspiration from single friends who were navigating the dating scene with very high standards. I combined their experiences with my own need for control and created a woman who's determined to set all the rules in a new relationship.

If you're curious about how this works in practice, you can check out my monologue "I Call the Shots" on YouTube. That monologue was the catalyst for my first major acting audition, which I booked. It showed me that writing characters for myself could be a powerful way to open doors in my career.

As you continue developing characters, ask yourself the following questions:

- What's the most uncomfortable situation I can put this character in?
- How does this situation connect with the genre I'm writing?
- What are this character's goals and motivations?
- Why is this character interesting to watch?
- Why am I the perfect person to play this role?

Development is key before you move forward. Your character and script need to be fully fleshed out before you start assembling your team or seeking financing. You have to be the train before you can convince others to jump on board. So, set yourself some deadlines:

- Create ten potential character ideas in the next two weeks.
- Pick one character and a genre by the end of the month.
- Commit to writing your first draft within three months.

When you show the world that you are the train, people will want to join you. You've got this. I believe in you.

CHAPTER 11

# WEAR ALL THE HATS: WRITING, DIRECTING, AND STARRING

Taking on the roles of writer, director, and lead actor in your own feature film is ambitious, challenging, and potentially overwhelming. While I generally advise against wearing all these hats for your first feature, I understand that sometimes you need to chase your dreams in a way that feels right for you.

However, having a solid grasp of each role before diving into all three can make the process more manageable. Consider starting with a short film and focusing solely on one role—be it writing, producing, or directing—to gain experience before committing to the complexity of juggling multiple responsibilities.

## The Challenges of Wearing Multiple Hats

When you decide to write yourself into the lead role, you're making a personal investment in your story. This choice can add depth and authenticity to your character but also requires careful consideration and preparation. Here's how to navigate this journey:

1. **Writing mode:** Start with the mindset of a writer. Your main focus is to create a compelling script that resonates with audiences. While you might think about budget constraints during the writing process, prioritize crafting a narrative that is engaging and well structured. By writing yourself into the lead role, you ensure not only that the character is relatable but also that the role plays to your strengths as a performer.
2. **Producer mindset:** Once your script is solid, switch gears to think like a producer. Like we discussed in the chapter on producing, you'll need to analyze your screenplay for budget implications and determine what resources you have access to. This step is crucial because your script needs to be feasible to produce.
3. **Fundraising:** After refining your script from a producer's perspective, it's time to shift into fundraising mode. We'll talk more about this step in a later chapter.
4. **Casting yourself:** As both a producer and actor, you'll need to advocate for your role convincingly. If your story is deeply personal, it's likely you'll feel a strong connection to the character. However, be aware that some may suggest casting someone else. It's vital to trust your instincts and understand why you are the best fit for the role.

Note to reader on how to know if you are best suited for the role: If you genuinely believe someone else is better suited for the role or that casting someone else would bring significant benefits to your project, then by all means, go for it. But as you've likely gathered from reading this, I'm a huge advocate for choosing *you*! No one will ever give you a better opportunity than the one you can create for yourself. You know the care, attention, and detail you deserve, and you're the one who can craft a script that lets your voice shine brighter than anyone else could.

There are countless amazing actors out there, and no doubt you could find someone incredible to play the role. But if you're the one writing the script, finding the funding, and bringing the project to life, why hand over your dream to someone else in the hope they might do it better? Instead, take the time to ensure you're ready to give the role your all.

That said, you have to decide what feels right for you. For instance, I didn't act in my first feature because I wasn't even considering myself as an actress at the time. Looking back, I wish I had taken that chance—it would've been another credit as a lead actor. But then again, the film might have turned out differently, so hindsight isn't always useful.

If there's an actor who excites you so much that you feel they could bring your dream project to life—perhaps even more thrillingly than if you took on the role yourself—then go for it. The heart of what I'm sharing here is to follow whatever sparks the deepest passion and excitement in you.

Ultimately, trust your gut. If the idea of stepping into that role excites you, then go for it—you're capable of anything.

## Emotional Resilience

Engaging in this multifaceted process demands an extra level of self-love, vulnerability, and patience. You'll need to navigate the complexities of each role while managing the inevitable fear of failure and rejection. However, the rewards can be significant. If you successfully create something meaningful that resonates with others, the journey will be worth it.

As you embark on this ambitious path, take a moment to reflect on your readiness to wear all these hats. If you feel prepared, I'm here to support you and offer guidance on how to make it all happen.

PART II

# GETTING (AND STAYING) ON TRACK

CHAPTER 12

# SET AN ARRIVAL TIME

A big part of being the train is keeping things moving. When it comes to making anything happen, one of the toughest challenges is maintaining momentum. People get distracted, things come up, and even if someone genuinely wants to help, their personal circumstances can pull them in a different direction.

In our industry, especially for freelancers, everyone is constantly looking for their next job. If a project starts to look uncertain, people quickly pivot to focus on the more immediate and reliable opportunities.

But I'm not telling you this to scare you. I want to inspire you to realize how crucial momentum is to your success. Moving forward is everything—and that's where setting realistic timelines and sticking to deadlines becomes key.

Many filmmakers take years to complete a movie, and I totally get that. Making a film is incredibly hard. It requires a huge amount of work, and so many pieces need to fall into place. But the way I approach filmmaking, which is definitely not the norm and might not be for everyone, is to set deadlines and meet them—no matter what. For me, creating is the fun part, and I want to do it many times in my life. I want to create, finish, and then create again. To do that, I need to keep moving, quickly and consistently.

So, what does this mean? How is this even possible?

My recent comedy special is a good example. During the pandemic, when comedy shows were canceled, Kaela Crawford (an incredible comedian) sent me a message on Instagram. She asked if I would be interested in doing a self-produced stand-up special about motherhood and pregnancy with her.

At this moment, two key lessons I'd already learned—the hard way—flashed through my head and needed confirmation before I could respond:

1. **Don't say yes unless you can truly commit.** Your reputation matters, and your word carries weight. People will remember if you follow through or if you flake.
2. **If you say yes, be ready to keep the momentum going.** This requires dedication, grit, and showing up consistently until the project is done.

I said yes. I was thrilled at the idea of doing a comedy special about motherhood and excited to do it with Kaela, knowing I'd learn a ton from her. The first thing we did? Set a deadline. Without deadlines, you could end up working forever, with no clear end in sight. We decided to release the special on Mother's Day the following year.

What followed was a year of weekly (and sometimes bi-weekly) check-ins. We wrote jokes, tested them on each other, tweaked them, and performed them online while comedy clubs were still closed. Once the clubs reopened, we hit the stage three to five times a week. I had also recently become a mom. Let that sink in—it was a *lot* of work.

Initially, we envisioned creating a one-hour special, with each of us performing for thirty minutes. We also thought we'd need a large budget to pull it off. We didn't focus on the "how" too much; we just kept working. But we never let the momentum drop.

At some point, we realized we each had thirty minutes of material, but not every joke was worth including. That was a bit disappointing, but it's part of the creative process. Not meeting your initial expectations is okay. We adjusted our plan, decided to do fifteen minutes each, and focused on honing the best material.

Then the next issue arose—how much money do we need, and how do we get it? We pooled our resources and called in favors. We thought we'd need three hundred thousand dollars, but in the end, we each spent five thousand dollars, raised from our network. We made *2 Moms 1 Mic* for a total budget of ten thousand dollars. We wrote, starred in, and self-produced it. We even self-distributed it.

Now let's take a step back. Was this the original dream? No. We initially dreamed of a one-hour special picked up by Netflix, with a budget of three hundred thousand dollars. But guess what? We did it. We created a comedy special. We had an incredible year building up to it, and Kaela became one of my closest friends. We filmed two shows in one night, with over 160 people in the crowd. Standing on that stage, I knew I was living a lifelong dream.

It's important to allow yourself to be proud of what you create, even if it's not exactly what you envisioned. I'd rather finish something than wait endlessly for it to be perfect. By doing, you learn what works and what doesn't.

We didn't move the deadline. We didn't stop the momentum. And even when it felt tough, we didn't give up. We made something we're proud of—something that's funny, relatable, and worth watching.

We released our special on Mother's Day, just as planned, and even got press coverage—including a mention in *Variety*!

Here's my advice for any project, especially a film: Set realistic deadlines, stick to them, adjust as needed, and keep moving forward. Sure, sometimes life happens, and timelines may need adjusting. If the work isn't ready, it's okay to take a break, but the key is to not let that break derail the whole project. This isn't the last thing you'll make—it's the first of many. You need to keep creating to keep growing and learning.

Everyone's process is different. I give myself three months to outline and one month for a first draft. Why? Because the outline is everything—it guides the story, and once I have that, the script flows. I write quickly, without worrying about grammar in the first draft, and then go through several revisions before polishing. The outline, for me, is the backbone of the process.

But my method isn't the only way. You have to know yourself and your writing style. If you write more slowly, or if you have a full-time job that limits your time, structure your deadlines accordingly. The key is to set them and try to meet them. Be kind to yourself if you need to pivot, but keep going. Be the train that never waits for something or someone to keep it moving.

Here's another example: For our most recent feature film, Dan and I really wanted to cast this one actor—he was incredibly talented but a bit out of our reach. He was interested, but other projects with big budgets kept coming his way. He kept delaying his decision about our project. We didn't have the resources to wait, so we gave him a deadline. When he couldn't commit, we moved on. Sure, that actor went on to do bigger things, and it might have been tempting to wait. But realistically, he would never have had the time to fit our movie into his schedule. We made the right choice, kept the train moving, and ended up completing our third feature film.

Momentum matters. Deadlines matter. Keep moving, stay focused, and adjust when necessary. The key is to keep creating, learning, and evolving as you go.

CHAPTER 13

## FIND A CONDUCTOR: WHY A LINE PRODUCER MATTERS

When making your first feature, one of the most critical hires you can make is a line producer.

Similar to the way a conductor (not to be confused with the engineer, who is more of the "pilot" of the train) coordinates the daily activities of the crew and ensures the safe and efficient transportation of passengers and cargo, the line producer manages the budget, schedule, and logistical details of your film, ensuring that production runs smoothly. I highly recommend hiring someone who understands how to work within the constraints of your budget and who has experience with projects at your scale.

This can be tricky. I've had friends who are incredible line producers on big-budget productions offer to help me out. While I deeply appreciate their willingness to lend their expertise, they often think from a large-budget perspective because that's what they're used to. Unfortunately, that mindset doesn't always align with the constraints of a smaller indie production, which is why you need someone who truly understands your financial limitations and can work within them.

A line producer is someone you'll work with daily, so it's essential to find the right fit. Here's what you should look for in a great line producer or production manager:

- **A positive, can-do attitude:** You need someone who's solution-oriented and doesn't get discouraged easily.
- **Strong budgeting and scheduling skills:** They must be able to accurately estimate costs and build a realistic production schedule.
- **A solid network for hiring crew:** Connections are everything in filmmaking, and a line producer with a reliable network is invaluable.
- **Experience working within your budget range:** They should know how to stretch a dollar and prioritize spending where it matters most.
- **Excitement about your project:** You want someone who's genuinely passionate about your film and invested in its success.
- **Strong problem-solving and research skills:** They should be adept at finding creative solutions and conducting thorough research to navigate challenges effectively.

It's essential to avoid working with anyone who makes you feel small or like they're doing you a favor. Filmmaking is hard enough as it is. Surround yourself with like-minded, enthusiastic people who believe in your project. A line producer is one of the first hires you'll make, and their involvement can frame the entire production.

That's why this chapter is solely focused on this role—it's that crucial.

It's also possible for a very low-budget film that you become the line producer by taking on the roles below and hire a production coordinator or UPM, which will be a person who helps you make sure you stay on track as you line produce the movie!

Once you've finished your script, the next step is getting a budget and a schedule. Without these, you won't know how many filming days you'll need, how to cast effectively, or how much money to raise. Many filmmakers hire a line producer just to create an initial budget and schedule. This allows them to assess the feasibility of the project and make informed decisions before they start fundraising. One of the first numbers you'll crunch is how many days you'll need to shoot. This is often the most significant factor influencing the budget, followed closely by location. Every time you move locations, you lose time and money, so it's vital to account for this when writing the script.

Here are a few examples from my own experience.

> **First Feature:** We shot in just fourteen days and in many locations, which was incredibly intense. While I wouldn't recommend this compressed timeline, we managed to make it work despite the overwhelming pressure. The biggest challenge was coordinating the logistics and ensuring everyone was on the same page with such limited time. We also traveled to Las Vegas for two nights to shoot all the bachelorette B-roll. This required coordinating everyone's schedules to ensure the trip worked as well as finding an Airbnb that could accommodate everyone while staying within our budget.

**Second Feature:** We filmed over nine weekends across nine months, coinciding with my second pregnancy. While this schedule offered us greater flexibility, it also introduced a unique set of challenges. Managing the fatigue of pregnancy while maintaining crew morale and ensuring consistency in performances over such an extended period was no small feat.

Additionally, after COVID-19 hit, we had to adjust to a significantly reduced crew size—down from twenty-five to just Dan and me. This shift meant that we both had to take on multiple roles, which became a substantial source of stress. As my pregnancy progressed, I found myself increasingly fatigued during filming, and the state of the world, coupled with the fear of contracting COVID-19, only added to the pressure.

We also faced the challenge of writing new sections every month. Since we couldn't finalize the film's ending without knowing how the world would evolve, we took the story one month at a time, which was exhausting. Writing, filming, and editing each segment monthly created its own set of difficulties, particularly in keeping the location consistent enough to match throughout the film.

**Third Feature:** We shot for three weeks across two countries, the US and Mexico, with a budget more than triple that of our first feature. While the larger budget allowed for enhanced production value, it also introduced new challenges, including the need to navigate different regulations, cultural differences, and logistical issues. In Mexico, we worked with a different line producer who understood the local landscape and spoke Spanish, which was crucial given the extensive movement between locations. Note I am Mexican-American, so I speak perfect Spanish as well but needed a local line producer to make every phone call on our behalf since there were a lot of moving pieces. Coordinating crew, extras, locations, and travel time in Mexico required careful management, so having someone who understood the logistics of getting from point A to point B was essential. Additionally, having a dedicated person in charge of managing extras was necessary in Mexico.

A skilled line producer is essential for keeping your film on budget and on schedule. They are your key to assessing what makes sense for your project, whether it's deciding how many shooting days you need or managing the logistics of shooting in multiple locations.

Hiring a line producer should be one of your first steps once your script is ready. Find someone who is good, reliable, and aligned with your vision because their guidance will shape your entire production journey. They'll help you keep the train moving forward, even when the tracks get a little bumpy.

CHAPTER 14

## DON'T STOP MOVING: WHY PERFECTION DOESN'T GET YOU ANYWHERE

The reality is that nothing you make will ever be exactly as good as you envisioned. That sounds harsh, but here's the thing: Anyone in a creative field has high expectations of themselves. In my experience, no matter how much money, time, or energy you put into something, most people end up slightly disappointed. That doesn't mean you don't like what you made; it just means you thought it was going to be slightly better.

Take a look at interviews with big-name directors. It's fascinating to hear them talk about not having enough time or money, even when they're working with hundreds of millions of dollars and months to complete a project. Their vision was probably so grand that, in their minds, the final product still didn't live up to their hopes and dreams. Instead of thinking they're ungrateful, I've come to understand a bigger concept. It's not about the money or the time—it's that we, as human beings, are always striving to create the best version of our work. Most of us are at least slightly perfectionist, critical, and judgmental, especially of ourselves. We are our own worst critics.

So, what does this mean? Are we never going to be happy with what we make? Kind of (just kidding!). But what's true is that letting go of perfectionism is essential to moving forward. My husband often gets upset when something doesn't turn out as well as he'd hoped, but when he watches it a few months later, he's proud of what he created. Time changes perspective.

I'm not suggesting you should just throw things together and hope for the best. You need to invest time and care into your work, but you also need to accept that the version you were able to make is the perfect one for that moment. Even if it's not exactly what you envisioned, there's value in what you've created, and there's always something to learn.

Let me share an epic failure story that highlights this. When I was studying at LMU, I directed my thesis film. At the time, I was into dark, intense films like *Requiem for a Dream*, *American History X*, and *Fight Club*. I wrote a short film about a woman in a controlling, emotionally abusive relationship, based on something I had experienced. In my ideal director scenario, I wanted the entire film to take place in one room, with the color of the walls slowly changing from vibrant to black and white, symbolizing how the male lead was draining the female lead's life of color. It's a beautiful metaphor, right?

Well, I hadn't considered how long it takes to paint a wall. Instead of having ten subtle color variations, we had three, and the final film made it look like my characters were constantly in different locations. Total fail. None of my vision made it to the screen. But here's the thing—I still made a good short film. It was my first short and the first thing I ever directed. And guess what? I'm proud of myself for being bold and trying something unique, even though it didn't turn out the way I'd hoped. I learned so much from that experience, and it led to more opportunities.

One of the keys to success is cultivating a culture of experimentation. It's about embracing the joy of learning and not letting your "not good enough" voice stop you from creating. It's okay if it's not perfect—nothing is. Even your favorite movie in the world isn't perfect. *Merriam-Webster* dictionary defines *perfect* as "being entirely without fault or defect," which, by nature, is impossible. So, let's move beyond that mindset. Let's focus on creating something exciting, inspiring, and authentic—and be kind to ourselves along the way.

## CHAPTER 15

## KEEP THE RIDE SMOOTH: STRUCTURING YOUR BUDGET

When we set out to make our first feature film, we had just thirty thousand dollars in savings. We made the decision to put it all toward the project, determined to figure out how to create a feature film on such a small budget.

Our first step was to be up front with our crew. We explained that everyone's role would involve shared investment; instead of a typical paycheck, everyone who worked on the film would receive a share of the profits. In essence, they'd be investing their time as their stake in the project.

In the end, things worked out even better than expected—we ended up raising additional funds as enthusiasm for the film grew, allowing us to pay everyone. While our initial idea of a shared-profit structure didn't fully come to fruition, the concept itself is a viable option for low-budget filmmaking. If you have a modest budget like we did, finding a fair structure that works for everyone is essential.

Here are two structures to consider for low-budget productions:

1. **Back-end points:** Offering your crew back-end points means they have a stake in the movie, like any other investor. Time is money, so if someone is willing to invest their time, giving them a piece of the project can be a fair way to compensate them. Back-end points, often referred to as *points* or *profit points*, are a way for filmmakers to share in the profits of a project after the initial costs have been recouped. This structure typically comes into play after the film has covered its production and distribution expenses, allowing stakeholders, such as producers, directors, and actors, to earn a percentage of the net profits. These percentages can vary based on the individual agreements but generally range from 5 percent to 25 percent, usually of the producer's share of the profits, depending on the person's role and investment in the project.
2. **Most Favored Nation (MFN):** In an MFN structure, everyone is paid the same rate. For example, if you're working with a tight budget, you might pay everyone a flat rate a day, regardless of their role. This equality can foster a strong sense of teamwork and shared commitment.

Be strategic in hiring people who understand your budgetary limits and can work within those means. Filmmakers used to large budgets are often accustomed to more tools and resources. Early in my career, I once hired a very experienced cinematographer who requested equipment and resources beyond what I could afford at the time. I learned the hard way that hiring someone who was at a similar stage in their career and could work within my budget would have been a better match.

A valuable resource for understanding deal structures in the film industry is the Producers Guild of America (PGA) website. The PGA offers educational materials, guidelines, and resources that cover various aspects of film production, including financial arrangements and contracts.

Additionally, you might explore the Film Independent website, which provides resources, articles, and workshops tailored for filmmakers, including topics on financing and distribution deals.

Another option is *The Filmmaker's Handbook* by Steven Ascher, a comprehensive guide that covers a wide range of filmmaking topics, including contracts and profit-sharing arrangements.

For more specific legal advice, consulting a lawyer who specializes in entertainment law can be invaluable, as they can provide tailored guidance on structuring back-end deals based on individual circumstances and industry standards.

Low-budget filmmaking requires a spirit of appreciation and respect for everyone's time and energy. It's essential to make sure that each crew member feels valued, especially when their compensation may not match the level of effort they're putting in. Here are a few ways I show appreciation on set that don't break the bank:

- **Birthdays:** If someone's birthday falls on a day we're shooting, I make it a point to bring a cake and celebrate them. It's a simple gesture, but it lifts everyone's spirits and helps create a positive, team-oriented environment.
- **Thoughtful treats:** Whether it's a surprise round of iced lattes on a hot day or a six-pack of beer at wrap, little treats go a long way. I've found that cupcakes, energy

drinks, or any small gesture can create a positive atmosphere that feels inclusive and fun.

Another crucial component of running a low-budget set is communication. Open and transparent communication can help solve most problems before they escalate. Low-budget films often require people to wear multiple hats and work long hours, so it's essential to check in regularly. If you're working with an editor on a flat fee, for instance, or dealing with a long day involving extras, make it a habit to ask your team how they're doing. Not everyone is comfortable speaking up, so take the initiative to make sure people feel heard and supported.

The most important thing you can bring to set, though, is your energy, as we discussed in a previous chapter. Your enthusiasm sets the tone for everyone else. I walk onto every set with a smile, begin each day with a safety meeting, and thank every crew member for being there. When you express gratitude and show genuine enthusiasm, it creates a positive ripple effect. I've had many people tell me they enjoy working with me because of my energy and the positivity I bring to set. People want to be part of an uplifting experience, and there's no better way to set the tone than with your attitude. Stress is inevitable on set, but approaching challenges positively goes a long way, especially in a low-budget environment where stakes are already high.

CHAPTER 16

# USE THE TRACKS YOU'VE GOT

Using the "tracks I have" is how I've brought every single project of mine to life. Usually, the first thing I do is think about the story I want to tell and why it matters to me. But as I begin building the narrative, I also make a list of everything I have access to. That list stays in my mind as I write the script, informing the choices I make.

Thinking about what you have access to can take many forms. For example, while creating my second film, *Single Mother by Choice* (available to watch on Max, formerly HBO Max), I knew I wanted to get pregnant, but I also knew it would be harder to get cast as an actress once I was visibly pregnant. So, I decided to use my pregnancy in the film. My husband suggested we film once a month throughout my pregnancy, tracking it in real time like *Boyhood*. I wrote a script with a pregnant character in mind, and we adjusted the script every month based on how I was feeling at the time.

Never in a million years did I imagine I would have a miscarriage—a heartbreaking experience that became one of the hardest things I've ever gone through. It took me a while to recover emotionally, but eventually, we decided to keep going. We stayed on track, kept being the train, and resumed filming. I even included the miscarriage in the story because I realized how important it was to talk about. I had felt so alone when it happened to me, and I wanted others to know they weren't alone.

Three months later, as we were finishing the "before pregnancy" portion of the film, I discovered I was pregnant again. And then, just as we prepared to continue filming, the global pandemic hit.

Imagine this for a second: I had just experienced a miscarriage while filming a movie about being pregnant. After much soul-searching, I decided to keep going and include the miscarriage in the film. Then I found out I was pregnant again, a total surprise. Now we had to keep filming because I was going to start showing soon. We were filming one long weekend a month to capture the real-time growth of my belly, which was a logistical nightmare. Getting the same crew together once a month was tough, and then—three months into filming—the global pandemic hit.

I don't know if you remember the intensity of that time as clearly as I do (I was pregnant!), but it felt like the zombie apocalypse. Productions were shut down. No one left the house. As a pregnant woman, I was allowed to see no one. It was terrifying.

But then we realized that something unique was happening. We didn't know how it would end or if we'd even survive. We didn't know if I'd get to have my baby. But we decided to keep filming. We were determined to be the train and keep moving forward. If nothing else, at least we'd be doing what we loved.

Looking back, I think, *What a crazy idea*. But it was also bold, brave, and the only way forward. We had no choice but to keep going.

We ended up rewriting the movie as we filmed. The original narrative was about two friends who decided to have a baby together because they hadn't found the right partners. It was supposed to be a fun exploration of friendship and the complications of raising a child together. But with the pandemic, we couldn't keep that narrative for two reasons:

1. I couldn't be around anyone because I was pregnant, and there was no vaccine yet.
2. My co-lead, Brittany S. Hall, had moved to a different city to be with her family during the pandemic.

So, what were we going to do?

Talk about using the resources you have. We bought an old camera from a friend, my husband took a cinematography class from our DPs, and he became the cameraman, director, and sound guy. I took on production design, acting, writing, wardrobe, and makeup. We went from a crew of twenty-five to a crew of two. It was the only way to keep going. And we decided the global pandemic would have to be part of the movie to make it make sense.

We rewrote the first three months of footage we had already shot. Unfortunately, more than half of it didn't make the final cut, which was a bummer and a waste of money. The new story was about a woman who wanted to have a baby with her best friend, but the pandemic forced her to do it on her own. It wasn't as funny as the original concept, but it was what we had available—and the only way to keep filming.

Our friend Anna Campbell was a huge help. Originally engaged as an acting coach, she became our producing partner and would jump on Zoom calls with us each month to help brainstorm what we could write and shoot next. We couldn't have a finished script because we had no idea what was going to happen in the world, when the pandemic would end, or even if we would be around to finish the film.

I remember one call with Anna where she kindly said, "Selina, you know you can stop if you want to. No one would blame you." I cried when she said that, because I needed to hear it. I knew I could stop working on the project, but I also knew that I wouldn't feel good about quitting. I genuinely wanted to finish.

So, we kept going. Every month, we wrote, produced, shot, and edited. We included real-world events, like the George Floyd protests. But this was still a fictional narrative, and let me tell you, I was exhausted.

At one point, after we finished the first cut of the film, we showed it to some friends, and they suggested it would work better as a short film. That hurt. They didn't mean it to, but it stung after all the emotional investment we'd made. I hired an editor to cut it as a short, and I watched it. Then I watched our rough cut. My husband and I both agreed: This deserved to be a feature. It needed work, but we weren't afraid of the work. So, we did it.

By the time we finished, I had given birth to our son, and we were still deep in the pandemic. We started shopping the film around. Most people said, "No one wants to watch a pandemic movie." We got one bad offer and almost took it, but Doug, bless him, told us to wait. So, we did, trusting that something better would come.

A few weeks later, Doug called with the best news: HBO wanted the movie—and they were offering double what we had invested. We were floored.

It turned out that because no one had been in production, there wasn't much to buy. Our film, shot during the pandemic, became a time capsule of the world during that time, told through our experience. And guess what? A lot of people had been pregnant and experienced miscarriages during the pandemic, and they could relate.

We also made an executive decision to skip the festival circuit. Everything was online at the time, and we figured it wasn't worth the risk. The film was timely, and we didn't want to wait too long to release it.

Reflecting on the experience now, I realize how rewarding it was. It was hard, chaotic, and filled with self-doubt, but we kept going. We even made a behind-the-scenes documentary short about the process, and HBO bought that, too. You can watch both on Max!

The point is that you can use whatever's in front of you. Life presents challenges, and movies are about life. Flexibility is key, but so is following your gut. Write what you have available and make the best story with what you have. You can do this. It takes grit, but you've got it. Don't let anything stop you from telling your story.

CHAPTER 17

# BLOW YOUR OWN HORN: COLD-EMAIL OUTREACH

This is one of my favorite chapters because I can confidently call myself the Queen of Cold Emails. I have probably sent thousands of them, and I'm not exaggerating! After years of doing this, I've learned what works, what doesn't, and how to craft an email that gets results.

There are a few key aspects to cold emails that are crucial for success, and I'm going to walk you through how to write a great one!

## Do Your Research

The first rule of cold emailing is research. Before you reach out to anyone, make sure you've done your homework. Do *not* email someone about something that is clearly outside their expertise or interest.

For example, I often receive cold emails from people asking if I would finance their horror movie. To start, I'm not a financier, and on top of that, I've never worked on a horror film—so right off the bat, that email is not relevant to me. Now, if someone reaches out saying they're working on a dramedy and need a connection to a great editor, I'm much more likely to respond. Why? Because dramedy is my genre, and the ask is something I can genuinely help with.

So, always make sure you're asking the right person for the right thing. Consider where you are in your career and what feels like an appropriate request. Sending a thousand cold emails asking for financing for your first feature is unlikely to work because, realistically, people don't give large sums of money to strangers for their debut project. Even if you and I both know you're going to make a killing, most people don't like the idea of potentially losing money.

So, the first thing I always do is targeted research. I ask myself:

1. What do I want?
2. Who can help me?
3. Why would they want to help me?

After answering these questions, I create a strategic list. For instance, I'm currently working on getting a Latinx TV show out into the market. I started by writing down every show I feel is similar in tone or has characters or themes that align with mine. Next, I found out who the showrunners were, looked up their agents or managers on IMDbPro, and compiled all the information in a Google spreadsheet.

Once I have my list, I'm ready to start drafting my emails.

**Be Specific**

For each email I send, I include one specific sentence that is only relevant to that person—something I genuinely admire about them or their work. It's easy to send a generic email, but if someone has taken the time to watch your work and comments on it in a way that's specific and honest, that changes everything. Whenever I receive an email from someone who has clearly seen my work and has something meaningful to say about it, I always respond.

If you want someone to take the time to help you, you need to take the time to watch their work.

## Find Mutual Connections

Whenever possible, I look up mutual connections through Facebook, LinkedIn, Instagram, and IMDbPro. This makes a huge difference because it turns you from a complete stranger into someone with a shared connection, which immediately builds trust.

Receiving an email from someone I don't know is one thing. But if they can say, "You might not know me, but Sandra speaks highly of you" or "I know you worked with Gary; I did too," that creates common ground. Now we're no longer strangers—we're one step removed.

## Mention the Benefits

When crafting your email, make it clear how helping you benefits them. For example: "I'm looking to hire a production designer and was wondering if you could connect me with yours from this movie." This is a simple, straightforward ask that makes the person feel good about sharing their network. Or "I have a fully finished film and am looking for distribution. Would you or your team like to take a first look before we go to market?" Here, they feel like they might be part of something exciting before anyone else has seen it. Always frame your request in a way that shows how it could benefit the other person.

Be specific about your ask, too. *Never* send vague requests like "Hey, I love your work—want to grab coffee?" It's not specific, it doesn't have a timeline, and most people are busy with their own lives. If your request can't be easily fulfilled, the answer will likely be no.

## Be Prepared

Before you ask for anything, make sure you've done the work. If you want money, have a budget and an investor deck ready. If you're attaching an actor to a script, ensure the script is finished. If you're looking for a producer for a show, have a detailed deck to present. You get the idea—prepare everything in advance before making the request.

## Present Yourself Well

Always present yourself in the best possible light. Don't frame yourself as inexperienced or green. For example, don't say, "I've never done this before and would love some help figuring it out." That makes you sound like you haven't done the work.

Instead, frame yourself professionally. For example: "I would deeply appreciate any referrals you might have." This presents you as someone who is capable, prepared, and ready to move forward.

## Write a Strong Subject Line

The subject line is crucial—it's what determines whether your email gets opened. Make sure it grabs the recipient's attention. For example, if I'm pitching a new Latinx TV show, my subject line might be something like this:

> [PROJECT TITLE] / NEW LATINX TV SHOW BY EMMY-WINNING PRODUCER/FIRST LOOK

Now imagine if I had written something more like this:

LOOKING FOR SOMEONE IMPORTANT TO HELP ME MAKE MY SHOW

Which one would you be more excited to open? The first one, right? So, always craft a subject line that excites the reader to open your email—it's just as important as the content inside.

**Don't Focus on Rejection**
You will mostly get no response. That's the name of the game. Out of the thousands of cold emails I've sent, do you know how many have replied? Probably less than a hundred. But it doesn't matter, because the ones who did respond led to amazing opportunities.

**Example Emails**
The following are some real-world examples of cold emails that led to successful outcomes.

The emails were written at different points in my career. I'm now at a place where I have an Emmy-winning producer attached to my projects, but I of course didn't start out that way. The point is that you should make sure that *anything* that can be highlighted to draw positive attention and credibility to the project should be highlighted in the subject line.

Note also that the first two initial approaches were ultimately written and sent by my assistant, though I initially drafted both. If you don't have an assistant, you might consider sending initial emails like these as if you do. I also added two emails that were sent from me directly before I had an assistant so you can see the difference in how it feels and how it can still work. Do what you think makes the most sense for you.

As you go through them, note the strategic tone, specific personalization, and clear calls to action that drive responses. I'll also share tips on why these emails worked and how to adapt them for your own projects.

## Example 1: Cold Email to Connect with a High-Profile Showrunner

> **Subject:** [TITLE OF PROJECT] / NEW LATINX TV SHOW BY EMMY-WINNING PRODUCER / FIRST LOOK
> **Email:** Hi [name],
>
> My name is Akasha, and I'm reaching out on behalf of writer and creator Selina Ringel and two-time Emmy Award–winning executive producer Angela Guice.
>
> We've been huge fans of Jenji Kohan's work, especially her groundbreaking storytelling on *Weeds*. We feel that [Project Title], the project we're currently developing, aligns with her sharp, character-driven narratives and unique voice.
>
> Small world, Selina had the pleasure of working with Graham Sibley and Gerry Bednob. Graham worked on Jenji Kohan's *Glow* and Gerry on her *Mad About You*.
>
> We're currently going out to showrunners and looking to attach talent soon.
>
> We'd love to set up a quick coffee meeting to share more about [Project Title]. We've included our deck, if

Jenji would be interested. Let me know when she has some availability?

Looking forward to hearing from you!

**Response:** Will send to Jenji—thank you.

**Why this worked:**

1. **Personalization:** The reference to Jenji Kohan's work and mutual acquaintances immediately creates a connection.
2. **Clear call to action:** The request for a quick coffee meeting is specific and actionable.
3. **Professional yet friendly tone:** Strikes a balance between formality and approachability.

## Example 2: Cold Email for a Brand Collaboration

**Subject:** You, Me & Her—Perfect Brand Collaboration
**Email:** Dear [Brand Name] Team,

My name is Jessy, reaching out on behalf of the producers of *You, Me & Her*, a new film set to hit theaters on February 14th. As part of our promotional efforts, we're creating "social lubricant" gift bags to include some amazing products that complement the film's themes—and we think [Brand Name] would be a perfect fit!

Logline: A chronically married couple flirts with a threesome to rediscover themselves.

[Link to *You, Me & Her* trailer]

We are having a wide theatrical release, and we're looking for brand partners who can help spread the word about the film while gaining some added exposure through our activations. We already have amazing brand partners like Pleasure Chest, Tierra Rossa, Simmr Dating app, Lalo Tequila, Zomoz Mezcal, Casa Selva, and Hotel Ysuri in Sayulita—just to name a few!

We're aiming to solidify impactful partnerships. Would love to jump on a call and discuss further. What is your availability like in the next few weeks?

Thanks so much,

Jessy

**Response:** Hey Jessy,

I sincerely apologize for the delayed reply and would love to learn more!

What does your schedule look like this week? I'm generally available most days except Monday at 11:00 a.m. and Thursday at 10:30 a.m. PST.

Looking forward to hearing back from you soon!

**Why this worked:**

1. **Compelling offer:** The brand partnership opportunity is enticing, given the high-profile partners already involved.
2. **Clear logline and purpose:** The quick film description helps the recipient understand why their brand aligns with the movie.

3. **Direct ask:** The email includes a request for a meeting, which helps move the conversation forward.

Here is a follow-up email I sent after our initial call when I hadn't heard back from them for a while. I had already sent an email outlining our potential collaboration based on the details from our call but had received no response. Two weeks later, I followed up with this message.

> **Email:** Hi [Name]!
> Just wanted to touch base and make sure you got our email? Do you want to do a follow-up call this week or next?
> Looking forward to chatting more :)
> Warm regards,
> Selina

**Response:**
Hey Selina!
I got your email but didn't get a chance to give it proper attention. I'll take a look at it tomorrow and run it up the ladder, then we can schedule another call for the end of the week.
How does that sound?
Cheers,
[Name]

**Why this worked:**

1. **Polite reminder:** It gently confirms receipt without implying urgency or frustration.

2. **Clear call to action:** It proposes specific next steps, inviting a follow-up call while offering flexibility in timing.
3. **Friendly tone:** It maintains a warm, positive tone, which is approachable and professional, keeping the door open for collaboration.

## Example 3: Cold Email to an International Sales Agent

**Subject:** INTERNATIONAL SALES AGENT/YOU, ME & HER

**Email:** Hello [Name],

My name is Selina Ringel, and you were referred to me by [Name]. We have an award-winning (13 awards), critically acclaimed (100% on RT), Latinx, LGBTQ feature film called *You, Me & Her*. We are gearing up for an eventized theatrical release in January–February and have partnered with various brands such as Lalo Tequila, ZOMOZ Mezcal, Pleasure Chest, PleasureMed, Tierra Rosa, and various hotels in Sayulita and San Pancho for giveaways.

[Link to *You, Me & Her* trailer]

[Link to marketing deck]

We have locked in our domestic distributor and are currently looking for an international sales agent to help expand our reach globally. Would you be interested in watching the film? We are also hosting our first event August 22nd at PleasureMed if you would like to come in person?

[Link to August 22 event]
I'd also love to set up a call to discuss this further. Do you have any availability in the next week or two for a call?
Warm regards,
Selina

**Response:** Hi Selina,
Thank you for your email. Yes, please send over a screener and we'd be happy to take a look.
Best,
[Name]

**Why this worked:**

1. **Warm introduction:** Referring to someone we both know provides an immediate sense of trust.
2. **Social proof:** Mentioning awards, a high Rotten Tomatoes score, and prominent partners builds credibility.
3. **Multiple action points:** The recipient can either attend the event or view the screener, offering flexibility in how they engage.

## Example 4: Seeking Representation

**Subject:** SEEKING AGENT // MULTI-HYPHENATE LATINX TALENT // SELINA RINGEL
**Email:** Hi [Name],

My name is Selina Ringel. I'm a multi-hyphenate Latinx actress, writer & producer currently represented by Mojo Management. I have a lot of projects getting off the ground and need an agent.

Here are some links to my work *[AUTHOR'S NOTE: Make sure the links work! If you're interested in following the links here, I've included the URLs in the Resources section.]*:

[Link to Selina Ringel stand-up set]
[*Tuning In* trailer (miniseries on Amazon)]
[Link to *The Best People* first feature trailer]

A little about my career thus far:

I was recently selected for HBO & The Academy's Tomorrow's Filmmakers Today program.

My first feature film *The Best People* was distributed by Samuel Goldwyn Films and is available on Amazon Prime & Tubi in the U.S.

I wrote, produced & starred in an eight-episode comedy series called *Tuning In*, available on Amazon Prime.

[Add further career highlights here...]

If you're interested in connecting, I'm available via Zoom anytime!

Hope you're staying safe and healthy.

Best,
Selina

**Response:** Hi Selina,

Send me a text with your first/last name. My cell is [phone number]. I'll call you when I have a few minutes open.

**Why this worked:**

1. **Professional summary:** I highlighted my credentials, emphasizing my experience and successes.
2. **Concision and call to action:** Provides key information without overwhelming the reader and ends with a clear invitation to connect.

## Key Tips for Effective Cold Emails

- Send it and forget it. Once you send an email or message, let it go. Set a reminder to follow up in two weeks, and until then, forget about it. Don't wait anxiously—put your energy into something else.
- Follow the rule of three. If someone hasn't responded after three attempts (spaced out by at least two weeks each), move on. They're either not interested or too busy, and that's okay. Focus on the people who want to be part of your journey.
- Personalization is key. Always tailor your email to the recipient's interests or work. Find common ground, like a shared contact or project style.
- End with a question. This increases the likelihood of a response.
- Offer a clear call to action. Whether it's a meeting, call, or screener, give them a simple next step.

- Follow up. Don't be afraid to send polite follow-up emails if you don't hear back, but respect their time and space. Follow up three times, spaced apart by two weeks each time. If you haven't heard back by the third time, move on.

By strategically crafting these types of cold emails, I've secured distribution, brand partnerships, talent attachments, and even management representation. Use these as templates to build your own connections, and never underestimate the power of a targeted, well-written cold email!

CHAPTER 18

# MAKING REAL CONNECTIONS—NETWORKING IS A BAD WORD

As a filmmaker, you're probably constantly hearing that you need to "network." I know I was!

*Networking* is this buzzword that's thrown around like it's the golden ticket to success. But here's the thing: "Networking" sounds transactional. It's often framed as a series of moves to make, as if you're building some transactional web where each person is simply a piece you hope to move in your favor. For new filmmakers, this is daunting because, let's face it, in the beginning, we are looking for a hand.

Meeting someone who shows interest can feel like a miracle. In those early days, I'd meet someone who seemed supportive, and suddenly I'd be holding my breath, waiting on that person's email or a coffee meeting that felt like it could "change my life." I remember that desperate feeling, believing this one person held the power of my entire future in their hands. But here's what I've learned: No one person will change your life. The only person who can do that is *you*.

When we approach people with a networking mindset, it shows. People can feel when you're in it for what they can do for you, and—news flash—that's a major turnoff. We're all busy, with entire lives outside of our careers, and people want genuine connection, not to feel like they're being used.

So, here's my take: Don't focus on networking. Focus on connecting.

## Practical Tips for Meaningful Connections

Connecting with someone means being genuinely curious about who they are as people—not what they can do for you. Most people who will help you along the way don't need to be coaxed or persuaded; they'll help because they genuinely believe in you and your work. Yes, you should absolutely ask for what you want—you won't get it if you don't ask!—but be mindful of timing, their situation, and how you frame your ask. Authentic connections lead to authentic support.

Curiosity naturally leads to friendship, and once that connection is real, asking for advice or support becomes a natural part of the relationship. When people care about you and are genuinely invested in your journey, you'll feel it. That connection feels completely different than when someone's only interested in what you can do for them.

Here are some tips on building meaningful connections:

- **Be curious and look for common ground.** If you're meeting someone you admire or who seems intimidating, remind yourself that you're just two people. Maybe you're both film buffs. Maybe you're both exhausted parents or you both hate washing dishes. These shared,

humanizing details remind you that they're a person too. When you relate as equals, conversations flow better, and connections become genuine.
- **Build relationships before you "need" them.** Don't reach out only when you're looking for something. Check in on people, celebrate their successes, and be there for them as a friend, not just a contact. This approach strengthens bonds and builds mutual trust.
- **Be generous in your kindness.** Offer value in whatever way you can. Sometimes it's encouragement, resources, or simply a listening ear. Be authentic, and people will remember how you made them feel.

When you're curious and approach people with kindness, you open the door to friendship—and that's far more valuable than an opportunistic encounter. Friendship is the foundation of trust, and trust is everything in this business. Those authentic relationships will help keep your train moving forward. Your genuine connections become the tracks that support your journey, not just "stops" along the way.

In filmmaking, as in life, we're all humans first. If you approach relationships with sincerity, respect, and interest, you'll find yourself surrounded by people who are invested in you—not just your project. And that's the kind of support that can truly change your career.

CHAPTER 19

# FINDING FUEL (PART I): FUNDRAISING FUNDAMENTALS

A lot of people reach out to me and ask for advice on fundraising. Let's face it—getting money is hard. Especially when your strength lies in creativity, fundraising can feel like a completely different skill set. It taps into the part of your brain that requires you to sell yourself, and that concept alone feels cringey, right? We don't want to *sell* ourselves—we're not products; we're people.

But the truth is, once your film is finished, it's a business. The goal is to sell it, and in order to start, you need money. Which means yes—you'll have to sell the *idea* of making your movie.

So, how do you do that? If you're not an established filmmaker with a track record of making profitable films, how can you promise that you'll deliver? And how can you assure investors that they'll see a return on their money? The reality is that you can't guarantee anything. No one can, not even the most successful filmmakers who've made millions with their previous projects.

But even without that guarantee, there are ways for you to get what you need. Here are some tips that I've found helpful when securing funding for independent projects.

**Be Excited**

People often think that film financing will come from traditional film financiers, but that's rarely the case, especially for first-time filmmakers or those working on smaller independent projects. Most film financiers follow certain "rules" about what they invest in—like name talent, genre films, or proven successes. When you're just starting out, however, anyone and their mother can be a potential investor.

What does this mean? It means you should be talking excitedly about your film to everyone, because you never know who might be interested in investing. I once had a laser hair removal appointment, and while chatting about the story I was working on (*You, Me & Her*), it turned out the doctor performing the removal owned the whole company and was excited to invest in the film. So, she did! That opportunity would never have presented itself if I hadn't been constantly and passionately talking about the movie.

Another strategy I use is asking people for advice, which can lead to them suggesting potential investors. For example, if I know a friend works for a company where a billionaire loves funding movies, I might say, "I'm looking for financing for my movie; any ideas?" This way, it feels more natural and less awkward than directly asking my friend to connect me with their billionaire boss.

**Be Prepared**

When talking about your project, here's the key: You need to be ready. If someone says they want to invest in you, you must have your script and investor deck prepared. While you can start talking about your project before you have everything ready, be mindful that sometimes interest fades. You could get someone excited about investing, but by the time you're ready to present all the materials, they might have moved on—maybe their second cousin convinced them to invest in crypto instead.

## Be Considerate

Think about the amount you're asking for and who you're asking. Let's say you need to raise one hundred thousand dollars for your feature film. Instead of asking one person for the full amount, you could break it down—maybe ten thousand dollars from ten different people. While ten thousand dollars is still a lot of money, it's more manageable for some people who have that kind of disposable income, and it feels like a smaller ask than the full amount.

Be mindful of your conversations and gauge what would feel comfortable for the person you're speaking to. I've had investors come in with twenty-five hundred dollars, which some might consider small potatoes, but for me, it was enough to pay for craft services for the entire shoot, so I was thrilled!

Also, check where you're shooting and what tax benefits might apply in that state. In California, for example, giving money to a film is tax-deductible. Highlight any potential perks to your investors that might make it feel more like an opportunity for them.

I also like to offer fun experiences for investors, like a day on set or tickets to the premiere with a plus-one. You have to be careful not to overpromise, as some things can get expensive, but some perks cost nothing and are worth offering. It costs you nothing to invite an investor to visit the set or to sign and gift them a printed script.

## Fundraising Platforms

Fundraising platforms can be an incredible tool for filmmakers because they allow you to connect directly with an audience that believes in your vision. They're not just about raising money; they're about building a community around your film before it's even made. These platforms let you share your story, showcase your passion, and bring others into the journey, whether they're family, friends, or strangers who align with your project's message. Plus, they provide a structured way to organize funding, making the daunting process of financing more accessible and empowering.

Several fundraising platforms cater specifically to filmmakers and creative projects, offering tools to raise money for films of all types. Here are some of the most popular and effective options:

1. **Kickstarter:** A well-known crowdfunding platform ideal for creative projects. It's an all-or-nothing model, meaning funds are collected only if you meet your goal.
2. **Indiegogo:** Offers flexible funding options and allows you to keep what you raise even if you don't meet your goal.
3. **Seed&Spark:** Designed for filmmakers, it offers unique tools like audience building and distribution guidance.
4. **Patreon:** Focused on ongoing support, allowing creators to receive monthly contributions from supporters.
5. **GoFundMe:** Great for personal fundraising campaigns, with no platform fee.

6. **Film-specific grant platforms:** Explore organizations like Sundance Institute, Women in Film, or Film Independent for grants and resources tailored to filmmakers.

Each platform has its own audience and advantages, so choosing the right one depends on your project's needs and funding goals.

## CHAPTER 20

# FINDING FUEL (PART II): VULNERABILITY IS THE KEY

You've probably heard the phrase *work with what you've got*. So, what do you have? You have your life experiences—stories and emotions that are uniquely yours. You have a reason for wanting to tell this particular story. You have a passion for the message you're trying to convey. You want to make an impact, to reach others who've lived through similar experiences. You want to connect. You need to know that you're not alone in your feelings and desires. That's why you became a filmmaker—because you have an overwhelming desire to share your art and be seen for it. You want to touch lives, to create something meaningful, and, in doing so, feel more connected to the world.

Here's my most important piece of fundraising advice: Wear your heart on your sleeve. Be vulnerable. Let potential investors know the real reason this story matters to you. Tell them why making this film is your dream and how it could change your life—and the lives of those who connect with it. (This is the director's statement we discussed as part of your deck in the directing chapter.)

Let me share a personal story to illustrate this. Remember when I spent a year trying to get my first feature funded for one million dollars and couldn't make it happen? That film was based on a short Dan and I did at AFI: *Real Love*, a parody of behind-the-scenes reality shows. At the time, I was really frustrated that we couldn't raise the money, and sure, one million dollars is a big ask, especially for two people who had never made a feature film before (and that's not to say you shouldn't aim high—you absolutely can!). But looking back, I realize now that part of the reason we struggled was because the project wasn't personal. We thought we were writing something trendy and relevant, something that fit into the zeitgeist, but here's a little secret: Don't write what you think people want. Scripts that are written for the market can feel inauthentic.

After we moved on from that script, I wrote a new one about two really close sisters—one getting married and the other struggling with the transition and fear of losing her best friend. It was deeply personal, because guess what—I had just gotten engaged to Dan, my business partner and best friend, and I have an older sister who I'm very close to. See the connection?

The point is, when you write something from the heart, it resonates with people on a deeper level. Our first project didn't have a strong "why." Investors need to feel like you care so much about this project that they'd be missing out on a huge opportunity if they didn't help you make it happen.

Vulnerability is key in fundraising—and in life—because people don't connect with the part of you that's trying to prove something. They don't connect with the version of you that seems polished and perfect. They connect with the part of you that's authentic, scared, and trying. The part of you that's sharing something raw and real. That's the part that inspires people to give their time, money, and energy.

Here's another story: I was invited to speak at a master class panel for Latinx filmmakers who had received grants to make their first short films. The students screened their shorts, and afterward, they pitched their ideas for full-length features. Most did a good job, but their pitches were largely focused on the business aspects—why their films would perform well in the market.

Then, one student stood up. Before playing her short, she quietly shared that her film was about homelessness and that it was very personal to her. She almost shed a tear as she spoke, and I immediately felt a connection. She didn't have to explain her personal experience—I could feel it. I got emotional even before the film started. Afterward, I pulled her aside and offered to connect her with people in the industry who could help. She hadn't asked for anything, but her vulnerability moved me to act. That's the power of being real, open, and authentic.

So, if you want to raise money for your film, don't be afraid to be vulnerable. Share your story, let people know why it matters to you, and they will connect with you on a deeper level. That's the key to getting support—and making your project a reality.

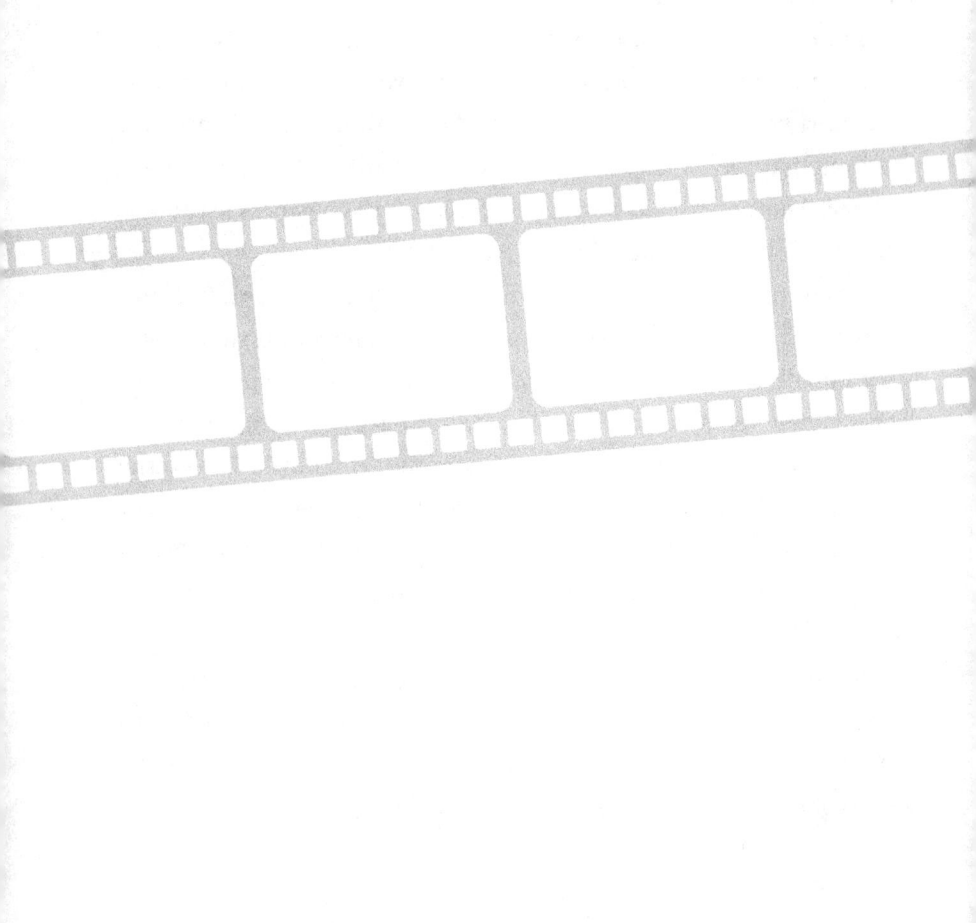

CHAPTER 21

# FULL STEAM AHEAD!: PRODUCTION

Starting a film project is thrilling, but the real test of your momentum comes during production and postproduction. Being the train means committing to constant forward motion, even when faced with logistical challenges, creative roadblocks, and the everyday chaos of filmmaking. Production and postproduction are about staying on track, ensuring that each element of your film works cohesively, and maintaining the energy and vision you set out with at the beginning.

**Casting**
Casting is one of the most crucial components of preproduction; it sets the emotional and narrative tone for your entire film. Choosing the right actors (which can include you!) can breathe life into your script, transforming written words into powerful, memorable performances. A skilled casting director can be an invaluable partner, helping you find talent that aligns with the film's vision and has the range to deliver authentic, nuanced portrayals. Not only do casting

directors streamline the process by presenting you with well-suited candidates, but they also understand how to assess a performer's chemistry, versatility, and potential for growth on set. Whether working with seasoned professionals or doing it on your own and discovering fresh faces, casting defines how your story connects with audiences. Investing in a thoughtful casting process brings depth to the film and helps create a collaborative environment from the very start—one where actors feel fully invested and in sync with your vision.

Something I like to do when working with actors, especially those playing family members or characters in close relationships, is to get them together for some shared time before filming. It can be challenging to ask for extra commitment when working with a tight budget, but if an actor has agreed to be part of your film, chances are they're eager to do their best. Spending time with their scene partners builds credibility in their role, making their character relationships feel more authentic and ultimately helping them succeed on-screen.

It's essential to ask for what you need while staying flexible. Focus on the nonnegotiable needs—choose your battles wisely. For example, in our film *The Best People*, we spent extra time with the two actresses playing sisters, encouraging them to connect outside of rehearsals. By the time we began shooting, they had their own inside jokes and a natural dynamic that brought real depth to their performances, making their relationship on-screen all the more believable.

**Communicating Your Vision**

As the director, you're the driving force behind the project's visual and emotional identity. To keep your train on track, you need to make sure your crew is not only aware of your vision but also actively invested in bringing it to life. This begins with crystal-clear communication and visual reference materials that keep everyone aligned. Make sure you have the following to share with your team:

- **A lookbook:** A lookbook is an essential guide that showcases your film's style, color palette, and overall mood. With stills from other films, color references, and concept art, a lookbook helps communicate the "feel" you're aiming for, giving your crew a visual road map. Your lookbook serves as a touchstone, helping everyone from the production designer to the lighting crew make decisions that match your vision.
- **Mood boards:** Mood boards expand on your lookbook by bringing in additional textures, settings, and design elements to inspire your team. This could include images of clothing, locations, props, and lighting styles. Mood boards help the production designer, wardrobe team, and cinematographer visualize the world of your film, ensuring each department has a clear understanding of the aesthetic foundation you're creating together.
- **Reference films:** Films that inspire the tone, pacing, or visual language of your project are invaluable references. If you're aiming for a Hitchcock-like suspense or the gritty realism of *City of God*, make that clear by sharing key scenes with your crew. When everyone is familiar with these touchpoints, it's easier for each department to deliver cohesive work that reflects the project's intended mood and style.

The more detailed your vision is, the better equipped your team will be to help you achieve it. Good communication isn't just about telling—it's about showing, inspiring, and guiding.

**Hiring Crew Members**
Once your vision is clear, it's time to build the team that will power your train through production. Choosing the right crew is crucial: These are the people who will shape your film's look, sound, and feel. Here are some key considerations when selecting your core crew members:

- **Are they already working on something else?** In the indie film world, it's common for talented crew members to juggle multiple projects. Confirm that your crew's availability aligns with your production schedule, and make sure they're committed to seeing the project through. A strong, dedicated team is the backbone of your film's success.
- **Do they have a support team?** On smaller-budget productions, it's not uncommon for crew members to operate without a full support team, which can lead to burnout or slower workflows. When choosing essential crew members like your cinematographer or sound mixer, assess whether they have access to assistants or additional resources that can keep their workloads manageable. This can help prevent potential delays and keep the crew's energy high.
- **Do you share the same vision?** Your crew members need to buy into the film's look and feel. Do they understand and align with the mood, themes, and

style you're going for? To gauge this, have candid conversations about their approach and share your lookbook, mood boards, and reference films. Your core team should feel excited about your vision so they can help you bring it to life with passion and focus.

## Keeping Production Going

Once you're on set, every day counts. Production is a whirlwind of activity, and keeping the train on track requires a careful balance of planning, problem-solving, and flexibility. Here are a few key responsibilities that maintain production momentum:

- **Effective scheduling:** Time is a precious resource, and an efficient schedule can make or break your production. Break down scenes by location to minimize setup and travel time, group similar shots together, and always build in extra time for unexpected delays. For example, if you're working in natural light, be mindful of weather and time constraints. A strong schedule allows you to maximize each shoot day, ensuring you don't get derailed by avoidable setbacks. A good assistant director can be a huge resource!
- **Quick decision-making:** On set, things rarely go exactly as planned. Lighting might change, an actor could get sick, or equipment could fail. When these obstacles arise, quick and decisive problem-solving is essential. Trust your instincts, stay focused, and keep an open line of communication with department heads.

Your crew looks to you for direction, so show confidence and adaptability when handling issues. Every solution keeps the train moving forward.
- **Strategic delegation:** Directors can't (and shouldn't) do it all. Your job is to maintain the overarching vision, not to micromanage every detail. Rely on your crew leads and empower them to take ownership of their areas. Delegating responsibilities allows you to concentrate on the bigger picture and prevents decision fatigue, which can quickly stall momentum on set.

## Switching to Postproduction

Postproduction may feel like a slower climb after the high-speed energy of production, but it's where your film finally takes shape. While it's tempting to relax, it's crucial to stay involved and motivated during the postproduction stages:

- **Editing: Shaping the story.** Editing is when the story truly comes together, and it's vital to approach it with an open mind. With your editor, watch the raw footage without judgment and be prepared to make difficult cuts or additions to serve the story. Stay receptive to new possibilities in the footage and let the edit evolve organically. Your editor is your partner in shaping the narrative; clear communication and mutual trust will lead to the best possible result.
- **Sound and music: Adding the heartbeat.** Sound design and music are not just finishing touches; they are the emotional backbone of your film. Choose a sound

designer and composer who understand the mood and tone you're after. Discuss the types of sounds, effects, or silence that best support key moments. Music should heighten the story's emotion without overpowering it. By treating sound and music as core components, you create a richer, more immersive viewing experience.

- **Color grading:** Bringing your vision to life. Color grading unifies your film's look, turning raw footage into a visually polished experience. A skilled colorist will help you establish a consistent tone that enhances the film's mood and atmosphere. Be specific in your direction here: Use the color palette from your lookbook to guide the grading process. Color is a powerful storytelling tool, and thoughtful grading will make your visuals feel intentional and cohesive.

## Finishing Strong

Postproduction can be challenging to finish as the thrill of production fades and the work becomes more detailed and meticulous. Here's how to stay motivated and keep moving forward.

- **Set realistic deadlines.** Postproduction can easily stretch on, especially if you're balancing other projects or running low on funds. Set specific, achievable deadlines for each stage—editing, sound design, color grading, and so on—and commit to sticking to them. Create a calendar to track your progress, and avoid perfectionism. Aim for a strong, complete film, not an endlessly

revised one. Knowing when to be done is essential to moving forward.
- **Embrace feedback.** Feedback is invaluable, yet it can feel intimidating. Seek out a trusted circle of colleagues who will give constructive input, and view revisions as opportunities to strengthen your film. That being said, you must also know when to trust your gut if you disagree with a note! Making a movie is subjective, but you must act as the ultimate decider—otherwise you risk getting stuck in an endless revision loop. Take feedback that aligns with your vision, and make revisions that you believe genuinely improve the film.
- **Prepare for marketing and distribution.** Postproduction is also the time to think about your film's future. Prepare for festival submissions by creating a compelling trailer, refining your synopsis, and gathering promotional stills. Build buzz by reaching out to festivals and distributors. Being proactive here can help your film find an audience and gives you another outlet for the excitement and energy you built up during production.

Being the train means staying in motion through production and postproduction, no matter the obstacles. Each part of the process requires focus, resilience, and the ability to keep moving forward. When you approach your film with energy, clarity, and control, you'll see your vision come to life—ready to share with the world.

CHAPTER 22

# JUST KEEP THE WHEELS TURNING: SELF-DOUBT AND CONFLICT

There's a lot of psychology in filmmaking because, let's face it, it's hard to keep pushing forward when it feels like you don't know what you're doing. And guess what? Most people feel this way at some point. As you gain experience, you'll start to build skills and understand the craft better, but every new project will still bring its own unique set of challenges. Every film is its own startup, with fresh hurdles and evolving dynamics among the cast and crew. A big part of filmmaking is learning to navigate through all of these unpredictable elements.

Two core skills help me stay steady on this track: the ability to push through self-doubt and the ability to resolve conflict.

## Embracing Self-Doubt

Self-doubt is one of the biggest challenges most of us face daily. If you don't feel it, that's fantastic—and rare. But for many filmmakers, doubt creeps in constantly, whether you're writing, directing, producing, or acting. The creative process is full of decisions that have to be made quickly and often with limited information, and it's natural to question whether you're making the right choice. After fifteen years in film, I can tell you that even experienced filmmakers struggle with what's going to work.

One of the skills you'll develop over time is listening to your gut. It's like a muscle that strengthens as you get more experience. At first, my gut was overwhelmed by fear—fear of doing the wrong thing, fear of making bad choices. But as I've grown to understand my tastes, values, and the types of films I want to create, I've learned to separate the noise of self-doubt from that deeper sense of knowing. Now, I can more easily tap into my gut reaction and feel confident in my choices.

When you're just starting, fear can overshadow your intuition, but pushing through the fear is essential. Over time, you'll see that even if you make a decision you regret, it's just another lesson. And sometimes, even choices you thought were mistakes end up leading to something unexpected and valuable. You won't always know what's working until the end, when it all comes together. And since art is subjective, what you dislike about your work might be something others appreciate. It's often the "imperfections" that make it great.

Remember, self-doubt is universal. Look at interviews with the greatest filmmakers—they all talk about it. Self-doubt is simply a sign that you care about the quality of your work, which is crucial. Instead of fighting it, make friends with it. That doubt is there to keep you accountable and honest, so embrace it as part of the journey.

## Developing Conflict-Resolution Skills

Navigating conflicts on set can be tricky, especially when two people strongly disagree. Typically, there's a clear structure of who makes the final decisions, but when both people have equal say, things can get complicated. For example, when Dan and I work together—he often directs, while I write and produce—we both have significant creative influence, but we don't always see eye to eye. Our perspectives can differ, whether about an edit, a shot, or a performance.

In these cases, we've learned that effective conflict resolution starts with truly listening to each other's points of view. Respect is key; when one person doesn't feel heard, small issues can quickly escalate. Another crucial aspect is putting the project above personal egos. This means letting go of the need to be "right" and focusing on what serves the film best.

One tool we use is called *mirroring*, a technique commonly used in psychology. It involves fully listening to the other person without interrupting, then reflecting back what they said to ensure you've understood them. This lets each person feel heard and can defuse tension. After you've mirrored back, they get to do the same for you. It's simple but powerful.

If you're at a deadlock, bringing in a third person for their input can also help. A fresh perspective can clarify the best path forward.

Sometimes, you may encounter someone who isn't doing their job well or is in a negative state that affects the team. In those cases, it may be best to replace them.

Deciding when it's time to let someone go from your team is never easy, but it's crucial for the health of your project. Start by asking yourself: is this person contributing positively to the work environment, and are they meeting the expectations of their role? If repeated conversations, clear feedback, and opportunities for improvement haven't led to meaningful changes, it might be time to part ways. Remember that your responsibility is to protect the project and the team's morale, even if it means making tough decisions.

Ultimately, most conflicts are solvable—especially if you choose collaborators with similar energy and goals. This goes a long way in preventing issues before they arise.

**Just Keep the Train Moving**
Whether you're grappling with self-doubt or navigating a conflict, remember not to get stuck. Filmmaking is dynamic, and stalling out because of inner fears or interpersonal conflicts can derail your project. Take the time to understand your feelings, express your concerns, and create a path forward. Conflict and doubt will always be part of the journey, but they don't have to stop the train. Instead, let them be challenges that refine your vision and make you a stronger filmmaker.

Remember, *you are the train.* Your energy and focus set the tone for everyone else on board. Bring positivity to the set, stay committed to your vision, and know that these challenges are all part of the experience of making something meaningful.

PART III

# THE RIDE NEVER ENDS

CHAPTER 23

# MAKING THE MOVIE IS JUST THE FIRST STOP

Here's the kicker, and one of the hardest lessons I've had to learn: Making the movie is just the beginning. Once that final scene is wrapped and the credits are set, the real challenge begins. Now, you need to get people to actually *watch* it, and I'd argue that's often the hardest part. So, if you're already skilled at social media, you're ahead of the game! Social media is becoming one of the most powerful tools for independent filmmakers.

Dan is fantastic at this. He's constantly strategizing how to engage people across platforms, build excitement for our projects, and create community by inviting others to engage with our content. For our latest film, he designed a creator's project where people could pitch us marketing ideas via social media videos. These creators got paid for their videos, and they earned bonuses based on the engagement their videos gained (like comments and shares). It's a win-win that motivates creators to try and make their videos go viral. Will every attempt hit? Probably not! But if even a few do, the impact could be massive.

We're in an era where traditional marketing methods don't work the way they used to, so innovation, disruption, and fresh thinking are key to capturing attention. Here's a guide on some core aspects of promoting your film and strategies you should consider, even as early as the planning phase.

## Social Media

Social media can be a filmmaker's best friend. It's a space to reach potential viewers directly, so use it to your advantage. Here's how:

- **Build anticipation early.** Start posting updates in the preproduction phase, sharing tidbits about your process, challenges, and small victories. Doing so creates a journey that people want to follow.
- **Post consistent content.** Consistency is key! Plan out your content calendar so you have a steady stream of posts leading up to the release, including trailers, teasers, cast interviews, and release countdowns.
- **Use platform-specific strategies.** Customize your approach for each platform. Instagram is great for visuals and behind-the-scenes moments, Twitter for updates and conversations, and TikTok for short, viral-friendly clips. Cater each post to fit the platform's strengths.
- **Foster engagement.** Encourage your followers to comment, share, and tag friends. Try hosting a Q&A or even a "director's cut" live stream where you answer fan questions about your film.

## Brand Partners

Partnerships can add serious value to your marketing efforts. A relevant brand collaboration brings mutual benefits and can broaden your audience. Here are some examples:

- **Targeted partnerships:** Choose brands that align with the themes of your film. If your film has an environmental angle, for example, partner with eco-friendly brands to access an audience already interested in those topics.
- **Cross-promotions:** Offer cross-promotional opportunities, like a co-branded giveaway or limited-edition merch. This gives both the film and the brand double the exposure.
- **Content creation:** Collaborate on unique content with a brand, whether it's a short promo, a contest, or behind-the-scenes videos that tie their product or service to the story of your film.

## Behind-the-Scenes Content

Audiences love a sneak peek into the filmmaking process. By offering behind-the-scenes content, you create more than just a movie; you create a world that viewers want to explore. Here are some tips for effective behind-the-scenes content:

- **Make it raw and real.** Don't just post polished clips—let viewers see the real challenges, funny moments, and even mistakes. Authenticity draws people in.

- **Include character insights.** Have your actors do brief introductions or character analysis, creating a deeper connection with viewers even before they watch the film.
- **Highlight the crew.** Shout out the people behind the camera! It humanizes the production and highlights the teamwork involved.

## Influencer Engagement

Influencers have dedicated followers who trust their opinions, so getting influencers involved in your film can be a huge boost. Here are a few ways to do so:

- **Influencer screenings:** Host a special screening for select influencers who align with your film's genre or themes. They'll be more likely to share their experience, giving your film social proof.
- **Collaborative content:** Invite influencers to create content inspired by your movie, whether it's a reaction video, review, or even skits inspired by the storyline.
- **Film ambassadors:** Ask influencers to join you as ambassadors of the film, posting updates along with you, sharing their excitement, and engaging their audience with the journey.

You might be thinking, "Well, this is great, but I don't know any influencers." Here's the thing: if you don't ask for what you want, you won't get it. Start by making a list of influencers who genuinely align with your film's message. Send them a DM on Instagram or reach out with a short, thoughtful message. Explain briefly why you admire their work and why they might resonate with your project. The worst-case scenario? They don't respond—but with a long list, you're likely to hear back from a few. Many people love supporting underdogs and meaningful projects, so don't underestimate the power of asking!

## Audience Participation

Inviting your audience into the process can create a deeper sense of investment; think of them as a part of the crew. Some ways to do so include the following (see also chapter 7 on crowdsourcing):

- **Crowdsource ideas:** Ask fans for feedback on certain creative choices, like poster designs or character names. This can be done through polls, and it gives people a personal connection to the project.
- **Fan contests:** Run a contest for fans to submit artwork, taglines, or even a short trailer, giving them credit or prizes for their contributions.
- **Live streams and updates:** Offer real-time updates, like a weekly or monthly live stream, where you discuss the film's progress. It makes fans feel like insiders.

## Journey Documentation

Documenting your journey isn't just content for now—it's an archive for future projects and proof of your storytelling commitment. Filmmakers can do this in a variety of ways:

- **Mini-doc series:** Consider creating a series documenting the making of your film. This could later be compiled as bonus content for streaming platforms.

- **Personal stories:** Share why this film matters to you. Talk about the journey, the hardships, the moments you wanted to quit, and the little victories. Personal stories resonate deeply.
- **Reflect on growth:** After the release, reflect on what you learned and how you grew. It not only closes the journey for fans but also sets the stage for your next project.

## Limited Theatrical Release

If feasible, a limited theatrical release can generate buzz and create a sense of exclusivity around your film. Even for a small indie film, there are some ways to coordinate a release:

- **Local screenings:** Start with local theaters or film centers. Promote heavily in those areas, reaching out to local press and social media for additional coverage.
- **Special events:** Plan special events, like a cast Q&A or a themed night at each screening. Make it an experience beyond just watching a movie. Think outside the box—what elements from your story can you use to create an experience for people beyond just the screening? Consider tying in themes, characters, or visuals from your film to make your audience feel connected to the world you've created.
- **Leverage press opportunities:** Local screenings can catch the eye of local news stations and film reviewers. Use this as a chance to build momentum and credibility.

## Festivals

Film festivals are often the gateway for independent films to reach larger audiences and gain credibility. Here are some tips for festival participation:

- **Festival strategy:** Select festivals that align with your film's tone, genre, or cultural focus. Don't just aim for the big names—target smaller or regional festivals where your film may stand out more.
- **Connecting (not networking) opportunities:** Festivals offer a rare chance to meet industry insiders. Use this time to connect with fellow filmmakers, distributors, and other potential partners. Remember chapter 18: You're making connections, not a network.
- **Publicity potential:** Festivals attract press, and even just an acceptance can be used as a marketing asset. Plan to maximize any festival-related press to generate more buzz.

The next chapter contains more detailed advice about types of festivals and how to submit.

By weaving together these strategies, you can transform your film from a completed project into a movement with a life of its own. Each part of this journey contributes to the bigger picture of getting your movie seen, remembered, and cherished. Keep building these "stops" along the journey, but remember, the tracks you lay down—the connections, innovations, and insights—will keep you moving forward on your creative path for years to come.

CHAPTER 24

# GETTING TO THE RIGHT STATIONS: FESTIVALS

Film festivals are a fascinating part of the filmmaking process. When Dan and I first started out, we were sold on the idea that only the big festivals matter, but that's not the full story. Festivals fall into different tiers of importance, and each can offer unique benefits to your film. Let's break down the tiers, starting with the most prestigious, to help you decide which ones might be the best fit for you and your project. Different festivals can bring different kinds of value to your film!

## Tier 1: Premier Festivals (A-List Festivals)

**Examples:** Festival de Cannes, Sundance Film Festival, Toronto International Film Festival (TIFF), Berlin International Film Festival, Venice Film Festival

These are the internationally renowned festivals, drawing major industry players, press, and audiences. Films that premiere here often get significant exposure, leading to distribution deals and even awards buzz.

- **Why submit:** Unmatched exposure and prestige. Getting into these festivals adds enormous credibility and often leads to press attention, distribution deals, and even awards nominations.
- **Competition level:** Extremely high, with tens of thousands of submissions and steep entry fees. These festivals are very selective.

**My thoughts:** First, these festivals only accept world premieres, meaning your movie can't have been shown elsewhere if you want to be considered. This sounds manageable, but waiting for one of these festivals can sometimes be a big decision. I had a friend who only applied to these six festivals with her indie film, hoping for the biggest shot. When she didn't get in, she ended up reapplying the next year to a different tier, which worked out for her, but she lost a year. This isn't necessarily negative—it's just a choice that has consequences. Though Dan and I have always dreamed of premiering at one of these top-tier festivals, we've come to understand the kinds of films they tend to select: larger-budget films with well-known actors. Each of these festivals has its own tone, and over the years, we've also learned more about our style and where we might fit. Remember that every submission costs money, so be strategic, especially if your budget is tight!

## Tier 2: Major Regional and Genre-Specific Festivals

**Examples:** SXSW, Tribeca Film Festival, BFI London Film Festival, Fantastic Fest, Annecy International Animation Film Festival, Telluride Film Festival, New York Film Festival

These festivals are highly regarded and offer a mix of industry recognition and regional or genre focus. Many of these have niches (for example, SXSW for edgier films or Fantastic Fest for genre films) and attract distributors interested in specific types of content.

- **Why submit:** Good visibility and strong industry presence, though not quite at the Tier 1 scale. These festivals can build valuable buzz within specific niches.
- **Competition level:** Still competitive but more accessible than Tier 1, especially if your film aligns with the festival's unique focus.

**My thoughts:** These festivals are still a huge accomplishment to get into, and if you make it, you should be very proud. They are also more welcoming to independent filmmakers, which is something to keep in mind. I recommend watching films that have previously been selected to get a feel for the tone and style they look for.

### Tier 3: Well-Established Independent Festivals

**Examples:** Raindance Film Festival, Cleveland International Film Festival, Seattle International Film Festival, Melbourne International Film Festival, Fantasia International Film Festival, DOC NYC

These festivals have strong reputations and followings, often spotlighting independent voices and emerging filmmakers. They can provide good press, critical reviews, and sometimes lead to regional distribution or direct-to-streaming deals.

- **Why submit:** Offers solid exposure within the independent circuit and a chance to build your film's reputation. These festivals are more accessible for emerging filmmakers.

- **Competition level:** Selective but open to first-time filmmakers and experimental or low-budget projects.

My thoughts: Dan's and my first feature premiered at Cinequest, which falls in this category, and it was an amazing experience with incredibly talented filmmakers. Many of them continue to make films and grow in their careers. For this tier, I highly recommend submitting to festivals you can realistically attend. Attending can make a big difference in terms of networking, so apply to festivals you can afford to get to without creating financial stress. Being present at these festivals can do a lot for your career!

## Tier 4: Emerging and Genre-Focused Festivals

**Examples:** HorrorFest, Nashville Film Festival, LGBTQ+ festivals like Outfest, ethnicity-specific festivals like Urbanworld Film Festival, Hot Docs Canadian International Documentary Festival, Austin Film Festival, Slamdance Film Festival

These festivals cater to specific genres, communities, or themes (for example, horror, LGBTQ+, documentaries, or screenwriting) and attract audiences with those interests. Many include panels, workshops, and networking events.

- **Why submit:** Great for reaching engaged audiences in specific communities and building a network within those niches. Some of these festivals also have distributor connections.
- **Competition level:** Moderate to low, depending on the genre or theme, often open to experimental or low-budget projects.

**My thoughts:** You'll know right away if your film belongs at one of these festivals based on its genre and theme.

## Tier 5: Regional and Local Festivals

**Examples:** Boston Independent Film Festival, Santa Barbara International Film Festival, Chicago International Film Festival, Maryland Film Festival

Regional and local festivals are great for building exposure within specific areas and can help connect you with dedicated, local audiences.

- **Why submit:** Allows for regional press and networking, which can help build grassroots support for your film.
- **Competition level:** Moderate, with selectivity varying by festival size. These festivals are generally accessible and can help build early momentum.

**My thoughts:** Building your audience at regional festivals is a smart way to create some initial buzz. These festivals can still be challenging to get into, but remember: "hard" should never stop you from trying!

## Tier 6: Micro-Festivals and Online Festivals

**Examples:** Online independent showcases, student film festivals, niche micro-festivals, YouTube- or Instagram-based festivals

These festivals usually serve very specific niches or operate online. They can be helpful for building a small, dedicated audience and are especially useful for newer filmmakers.

- **Why submit:** A great option if you're working with a limited budget and are looking for feedback, networking, or niche exposure. Some offer digital badges, online press, or even limited distribution.
- **Competition level:** Low to moderate, depending on the festival. A good fit for filmmakers still building their portfolio.

**My thoughts:** Micro-festivals are great for visibility and adding laurels to your poster. It can create a perception of momentum, and as much as we may want to downplay it, festival validation can help build credibility and attract more attention to your film.

* * *

Each tier serves a unique purpose, and depending on your film's genre, audience, and goals, one or more of these tiers could be an ideal fit for your festival strategy. Ultimately, create a budget for your festival submissions, then decide how many festivals to apply to and where you'll focus your energy. Look at your film's tone, genre, and budget, and consider where it will be most celebrated.

For example, I had a friend who got into Sundance with an amazing film. Even though she won a section of the festival, she couldn't secure press or a distribution deal. She ended up self-distributing, which is a great option, but as a smaller film at a massive festival, it was hard to get attention. Think about where you will feel most championed.

We once attended a festival that covered our hotel and flights. That VIP treatment made us feel truly valued and added so much to the experience.

## Distributors and Sales Agents

Distributors and sales agents can also play a crucial role in getting your film to the right audience (unless you choose to self-distribute, which is always an option).

My first feature film, *The Best People*, had a successful festival run with awards and a premiere at Cinequest, after which we partnered with a sales agent, who helped make the film available worldwide. However, a major learning moment came when we discovered just how high the recoupment would be for the sales agent before we saw any return. Although we were led to believe the recoup would come quickly, the reality was much slower. Most sales agents work this way, covering their expenses, including attending festivals and pitching films to buyers.

With this experience under our belt, we took a different route for *Single Mother by Choice*. Doug (who worked at Mojo Management at the time) facilitated a direct sale, leveraging his industry relationships. It's worth noting that distribution often requires connections that go beyond the standard cold email (although, surprisingly, our first film's sales agent did come from a strategic cold email!). The timing also worked in our favor, as the pandemic had created a demand for new streaming content.

Being the train sometimes means *not* moving forward if it doesn't feel right. We were about to sign a deal for our second feature, but it didn't feel good, and we decided to wait. It was risky, but risk-taking is integral to being the train. Ultimately, the HBO sale (2021) turned out to be highly successful, building the momentum we needed for our next project. By 2022, we were already shooting our next film, and we had fresh enthusiasm from investors to fund it—giving us the drive to quickly develop something new.

For *You, Me & Her*, we chose to reenter the festival circuit after skipping it for our previous film during the pandemic. Festivals can help build critical acclaim and prepare for distribution. When we were accepted to Dances with Films, we had a choice: premiere there or wait and try for SXSW, knowing the latter wasn't guaranteed and would delay the release by a year. Looking back, I'm still uncertain if waiting would've been better, but we opted to keep the momentum. Timing also matters because the energy to promote a film can dwindle if it sits too long.

Our Dances with Films premiere seemed promising—until the strikes hit a week later, halting all press and promotion for films with SAG actors. Of course, we support the strike's purpose, but it created a huge setback for us. Our festival run and publicity plans were now silent, and the film went unseen for seven months. How could we relaunch it when the industry had gone silent? We restarted from scratch, using saved photos and reigniting interest months later with a new strategy.

Meanwhile, the industry changed again. Streaming platforms reevaluated budgets, often limiting support for independent films. We felt the pressure and knew we had to innovate. So, we pivoted to brand partnerships, using events to drive attention. Through cold emails and personal contacts, we secured collaborations with brands like Lalo Tequila, Zomoz Mezcal, Hotel Ysuri, and others. We hosted events with unique giveaways—including a trip to Mexico, where the movie was shot—to spark conversations around the film.

During this process, my husband cold-emailed John Fithian (former CEO of the National Association of Theatre Owners), who had cofounded The Fithian Group with Patrick Corcoran and Jackie Brenneman. They saw our passion and innovative approach and graciously took a call with us. After following up persistently but respectfully, we invited them to a private screening. They enjoyed the film but didn't commit immediately.

After more follow-ups and a lunch meeting, we learned that The Fithian Group was developing something new—a cutting-edge digital theatrical marketplace and distribution platform called Attend. We proposed that they test this new technology, which would connect filmmakers directly to theater owners, with our movie. They agreed, and our film *You, Me & Her* became the first test for the platform. We built a partnership with them which opened up a theatrical distribution opportunity far beyond our expectations and with the potential to massively disrupt the industry.

This path wasn't easy. It took diligence, persistence, and knowing how to offer value in a way that met their needs. This chance will help us push the boundaries of distribution. If we hadn't tried every avenue, we wouldn't be here.

## Final Advice

Email the festival organizers, jury, and programmers. Go back to chapter 17 and remember that a well-timed, respectful email can help you stay on their radar. Programmers are inundated with submissions, so if you can make a memorable impression (politely), do it!

Try to attend as many festivals as possible. For *Single Mother by Choice*, we decided to skip festivals if we couldn't attend in person, because so much of the festival experience is seeing people engage with your work. Watching people laugh at your jokes or connect with your story is priceless—it means your art sparked a conversation, which is the dream.

To be honest, I don't know of many distributors or sales agents who attend festivals outside of Tier 1 and Tier 2. But even if they aren't present, attending festivals can help you get noticed and may open doors for you to reach out to them later.

Also, use FilmFreeway. FilmFreeway is a fantastic resource for filmmakers because it streamlines the festival submission process, making it easy to find and apply to festivals of all types and tiers worldwide.

Be sure to include a festival budget in your overall feature film budget, along with a bit of funding for travel to these festivals. It doesn't need to be an enormous amount, but it's wise to think ahead about these costs, as well as setting aside some funds for marketing. After every film, we've had to raise additional money to get to the next stage, and trust me, it's not fun to go back to investors asking for more funding just to keep your momentum going. Planning for these needs up front can make a big difference in keeping your project moving forward smoothly.

CHAPTER 25

# SURROUND YOURSELF WITH OTHER TRAINS

One of the most valuable lessons I've learned is that surrounding yourself with other trains—meaning inspiring people who keep moving forward no matter what—is one of the best things you can do for yourself. These people will elevate and motivate you.

Many people worry about competition, fearing that there are only a few spots for "winners" and that success is about staying ahead of others. But the truth is, there's space for everyone. While not every movie will get made, *your* movie is so unique that it's not really in competition with anything else. Why? Because your idea came from you, shaped by your unique life experiences and perspective. No one else can replicate that.

Beyond that, being surrounded by driven, hardworking individuals is incredibly motivating. There will be moments when you feel like giving up, but watching others push through will inspire you to keep going. Their success shows you that your goals aren't as far away as they might seem.

In fact, I started a women's group called Be the Train before writing this book because I was inspired by a few amazing women in my life. I realized they all needed to meet each other. The more we surround ourselves with movers and shakers—people who are actively creating and pushing boundaries—the more we can inspire each other and lend support. This group is filled with powerhouse women: One friend has won two Emmys, another is the president of NALIP, one wrote *Crazy Rich Asians 2*, and a few have directed features with multi-million-dollar budgets. A few of them have written, produced, and starred in features that have made it to theaters or streaming platforms. They are all incredibly talented and passionate, creating remarkable things in their lives every day. I'm truly in awe of each of them.

But what's crucial to note is that none of these people started with these impressive résumés. They've been trains for years—persistent, hardworking, and unstoppable. I've seen their dedication turn dreams into reality. It wasn't luck, but grit and determination. That's the kind of community you need to build around yourself. In the beginning, your fellow trains won't have long lists of accomplishments, but you'll see their dedication, and that will be enough to inspire you, just as you'll inspire them.

I'll never forget an experience that perfectly illustrates this idea. In 2017, after finishing my first feature, Dan and I went to the Cannes film festival to try to sell it. We wandered the streets of Cannes, ate great food, and tried to navigate the market, but honestly, it was a bit of a failure. We didn't know that many people or how to navigate the festival. We had drinks with friends who were busy assistants at different companies, but that was about it.

Cut to 2022: We returned to Cannes while raising money for our third feature, and it was a completely different experience. All those assistants from 2017 were now producers, CEOs, or decision-makers in their companies! Suddenly, we were getting invited to every party, meeting sales agents, and making connections with people who wanted to help us. Most new faces we met had friends in common with us, and we formed quick bonds. It was a total 180-degree shift from our first trip. What had changed? Everyone, including us, had spent the past almost six years working relentlessly. Surrounding ourselves with hardworking, gritty people helped elevate our own journey, both in terms of energy and opportunities.

This is why I believe in the power of mentors—and in being a mentor, too. You might be thinking, *How can I mentor someone when I don't even know what I'm doing?* But mentorship doesn't always mean having all the answers. In fact, some of the best mentors I've had have been honest about the fact that they were figuring things out too. We're all on our own journeys, but if you keep working hard, problem-solving, and connecting with others, you'll move forward.

If you've made your first feature, you can mentor someone who hasn't. If you haven't yet, you can inspire others to pursue their own goals. Mentorship is about offering support—whether emotional or practical.

Not every piece of advice you give (or receive) will be what's needed, and that's okay. I've had wonderful mentors whose advice I didn't follow, and that doesn't make them bad mentors. They still helped guide me by showing me options and allowing me to trust my own instincts. It's like when you ask someone which of two outfits they like better, and when they choose the one you weren't leaning toward, it only confirms which one *you* truly want to wear.

The point is, surround yourself with trains. Elevate yourself by connecting with people who inspire you, and inspire others in return. Ask for mentors and be a mentor. Be a friend who gives advice without judgment. Take the time to read others' scripts, watch rough cuts, or volunteer on set if you can. These acts are deeply appreciated, and you'll learn something valuable from them.

CHAPTER 26

# EVEN WRONG TURNS CAN MOVE YOU FORWARD

In filmmaking—and in life—failure is not the end of the road. In fact, it usually helps propel future success. Just like a train that occasionally takes the wrong track or encounters unexpected delays, failure is an unavoidable part of reaching your destination. Every setback teaches valuable lessons, providing the experience and knowledge needed for your next project. Without these moments of failure, growth and progress would be impossible. Each failure pushes you forward, making you stronger, more resilient, and better prepared for the next leg of the journey.

One of the biggest mindset shifts we need to make in life is how we view and absorb failure. Failure *is* success. Why? Because you have to fail a few times before you truly succeed. Failure is how you learn, grow, and get better. There is no other way! If you succeed at something on your very first try, well, you got lucky—and that's great! But to create a sustainable career, you need to try multiple times. And yes, failure will come, but that's not something to fear.

It's a learning moment. Every time something hasn't worked for Dan and me, we've learned something valuable.

So much of life comes down to how we frame things. If you believe failure is a bad thing, it will stop you from trying. But failing *is* trying. You have to try countless things, fail in countless ways, in order to start understanding what works. My belief is that everyone should be trying, constantly. Yet, I know so many people who, out of fear of failure, never start anything. But what are the real stakes? Sure, failing can feel embarrassing or make you a bit sad or anxious—especially if it's in front of others. But failing is like building a muscle. You have to go to the gym every day to get stronger. If you're too scared to lift the smaller weights because they feel insignificant, you'll never be able to pick up the big weights when it matters.

It literally takes months of lifting smaller weights before you're ready to lift the big ones. Success is the same. You need to build the strength to handle it. And the only way to do that is by living through the failures.

Dan and I joke all the time that we are "failing constantly." What we really mean is that we're constantly trying. Most things don't work, and that's okay, because they lead us to the things that *do* work. For example, right now I'm working on securing brand partnerships for our newest feature film's theatrical release. We're organizing unique, disruptive activations with different brands, and I've probably sent over a thousand cold emails. Think about that for a second—over a thousand cold emails (each one strategic and thoughtful, just like I discussed in an earlier chapter). Out of those thousand emails, I've solidified ten partnerships—ten authentic, integrated partnerships that will totally elevate our film's marketing effort and release.

I truly believe that failure is just another word for *trying*, and there is no success without it. So, get used to it, get comfortable with it, and even find a way to enjoy some of your failures. Along with money, it's the fuel that keeps the train moving.

CHAPTER 27

# ENJOY THE RIDE

Much like a train's adventure is defined by the sights, stops, and challenges along the way, your growth, learning, and creativity emerge during the journey. It's about embracing the experiences, relationships, and lessons that shape you, making the destination worthwhile.

One of the biggest and hardest lessons I've learned is that there is no *real* destination. I spent years chasing results—whether it was awards, festivals, money, prestige, or validation. But the reality is, when those moments finally come (and I've been lucky enough to have lived through quite a few), they're short-lived and don't linger the way you think they will.

If I'm being honest, my fondest memories aren't from standing on a stage, holding a trophy. They're from being on set, trying to figure things out. Those moments of problem-solving, writing the script, doing the table read, rehearsing, trying to find a location, and yes, even when the location fell through and we had to scramble. The sleepless nights, showing up to set deliriously tired but buzzing with excitement for that morning coffee, running entirely on adrenaline because your body insists you keep going, even when you think you can't. Those late nights after filming, watching dailies with Dan (yes, I'm lucky I get to do this with my best friend). The trips, the people I've met along the way, watching everyone around me grow, create, and shift. *Those* are the real memories—the ones that stay.

I remember when we sold *Single Mother by Choice* to HBO. Dan and I had a moment where we thought, *We did it! We made it. This is what we've been waiting for our whole career.* And it was! But then the reality hit: *We need to figure out what's next.* We had to do it all over again. And, of course, next time it had to be bigger and better. We wanted more, because that's how humans are wired, right?

Even when I've won awards (and don't get me wrong, I love an award—and getting dressed up for an award show!), life still happens. The next day, I still have to wake up and deal with all the usual things. Somehow, we convince ourselves that these validation moments will last forever, but they don't. We're always hungry for more. Every time we reach a milestone, we start looking at the things we haven't achieved yet, and that's the tricky part of the human condition.

But the real magic? It's in the *making* of the thing. That's when you're truly tapped into your creativity, and it's the most exhilarating part. You're that version of yourself who wakes up at four in the morning with ideas you *need* to write down. You're running on excitement, anxiety, and a lack of sleep, wondering if everything you're doing is worth it, if it'll go anywhere. It's terrifying and wonderful all at once. And it's the *best* part of the process.

A good friend of mine (who's part of the Be the Train group I put together) once told me a story that stuck with me. She was running a marathon, and all she could focus on was the people ahead of her. She felt behind, like she wasn't measuring up. But then she got so tired, she had to stop and take a break. When she did, she looked back and realized—there were so many people behind her. She wasn't at the end like she thought; she was in the middle. Actually, she was in the leading half.

That story was such a powerful reminder that we're all on our own path, moving at our own pace. Focusing only on the end goal actually blocks the flow of creativity. We can't control the results. We can't control whether we win the award or whether people like our movie. But we *can* control whether we enjoy the life we're living right now.

There's so much to be grateful for, even in the quieter moments. I find myself wanting more to do when things slow down, and then wanting less to do when things speed up. I'm working on just loving every phase as it comes. Some moments are fast and full of creativity—that's when you really feel like the train, powering ahead. And that's what this book is all about.

But here's the thing: You're still the train even when you need to take a break. You're still the train if your movie doesn't get into any festivals or doesn't win awards. You're still the train if your friends don't tell you it's amazing. Most people aren't out there being vulnerable every day, putting themselves on the line. But *you* are. And that's one of the biggest ingredients to being the train.

The other key? Being your own biggest cheerleader. People will love some things, hate others, and sometimes be completely indifferent. That's okay. That's not for you to take on. You're pursuing your dreams, and you're making things happen for yourself.

The destination is *nowhere*. There's no place you'll get to where you'll stop wanting more. I promise you that. So what does that mean? It means you need to start loving every day, every moment—whether it's good, bad, or filled with problems you need to solve. Take on each day with excitement. Let everything be fuel, because you are a train. You're moving in the direction you want to go, and the real trick is that there's no final destination. You just keep moving forward.

Sometimes you'll pause. Sometimes you'll speed up. But your life is the journey. Take the time to look out at the view, enjoy the people who surround you, and don't get stuck on what hasn't happened yet. Don't get stuck on where you need to land to feel proud of yourself.

Being the train is about giving yourself permission—right now—to be proud of who you are and what you're capable of. You don't need anyone else's approval for that. Once you truly believe in yourself, you'll be able to move mountains. And you will.

# RESOURCES

I want to share a few key resources that could be invaluable as you start building your film. Below, you'll find a selection of organizations that foster community and help you connect with crew as well as practical tools from my own projects. These include a low-budget indie film schedule and budget, a financing deck, a director's deck, outlines, and more. I hope these tools will serve as inspiration and guidance for your journey.

## Filmmaking Communities and Networks

- **Sundance Collab:** An online community offering courses, feedback sessions, and opportunities to collaborate with other filmmakers. Website: www.collab.sundance.org.
- **Women in Film (WIF):** A nonprofit advocating for women in the film industry through networking events,

grants, and mentorship programs. Website: www.womeninfilm.org.
- **Film Independent:** Known for networking events, educational programs, and support for independent filmmakers, including the Film Independent Spirit Awards. Website: www.filmindependent.org.
- **Stage 32:** A social networking platform for film, television, and theater professionals to build connections, find crew, and learn from peers. Website: www.stage32.com.
- **National Association of Latino Independent Producers (NALIP):** Supports Latino filmmakers with networking opportunities, panels, and mentorship programs. There are more of these for different niche communities. Website: www.nalip.org.
- **American Film Institute (AFI):** A renowned organization dedicated to educating and inspiring filmmakers through programs, resources, and a rich archive of film history. Website: www.afi.com.

## Crew and Production Resources

- **The Mandy Network:** A platform for posting and finding crew jobs in the film and television industries. Website: www.mandy.com.
- **ProductionHUB:** A comprehensive resource for finding crew members, from camera operators to production designers. Website: www.productionhub.com.

- **Staff Me Up:** A platform to hire production staff or crew members, especially for indie filmmakers and smaller projects. Website: www.staffmeup.com.
- **ProductionBeast:** A job board and networking site specifically for the film and television industry. Website: www.productionbeast.com.
- **Backstage:** A casting platform for actors and performers, offering audition listings and industry advice. Website: www.backstage.com.
- **Actors Access:** A platform for actors to submit to auditions and showcase their profiles to casting directors. Website: www.actorsaccess.com.
- **IMDbPro:** A subscription-based service that provides detailed information on the film industry, including access to contact details for professionals and casting calls. Website: www.imdbpro.com.
- **LinkedIn:** A valuable networking tool to connect with industry professionals in all departments. Website: www.linkedin.com.

### Financing and Budgeting Resources

- **Film Funding Club:** Offers insights and advice on indie film financing, including templates for proposals and investor decks. Website: www.filmfundingclub.com.
- **Indie Film Hustle:** Provides podcasts, guides, and courses on budgeting, financing, and film distribution. Website: www.indiefilmhustle.com.

- **Crowdfunding platforms:** Websites like Kickstarter and Seed&Spark are designed for filmmakers looking to fund projects through public support. Kickstarter: www.kickstarter.com. Seed&Spark: www.seedandspark.com.

## Screenwriting and Preproduction

- **WriterDuet:** A collaborative screenwriting software that allows writers to work together in real time. Website: www.writerduet.com.
- **Scriptwriting software:** This includes tools like Celtx and Trelby or industry standards like Final Draft. Celtx: www.celtx.com. Trelby: www.trelby.org. Final Draft: www.finaldraft.com.
- **Shot list and storyboard templates:** These are useful for keeping productions on track visually and logistically. (Various downloadable templates available online.)
- **Scheduling software:** Programs like StudioBinder or Movie Magic Scheduling help create shooting schedules and manage production timelines. StudioBinder: www.studiobinder.com. Movie Magic Scheduling: www.movie-magic.com.
- **Canva:** A graphic design platform useful for creating marketing materials and presentations. Website: www.canva.com.
- **The Tracking Board:** A resource for tracking industry news, scripts, and talent. Website: www.tracking-board.com.

- **Scriptshadow:** A website that provides resources, reviews, and coverage for screenwriters. Website: www.scriptshadow.com.

## Union and Nonunion Resources

- **Screen Actors Guild (SAG-AFTRA):** Provides information on union regulations and resources for hiring union talent. Website: www.sagaftra.org.
- **Film Independent:** Offers resources for both union and nonunion filmmakers, including workshops and networking opportunities. Website: www.filmindependent.org.
- **Casting Society of America (CSA):** A directory of casting directors and resources for hiring and working with them. Website: www.castingsociety.com.

## Production Legalities

- **Entertainment lawyers:** Look for legal resources through websites like Lawyers for the Arts, which provides access to counsel experienced in production law. Website: www.lawyersforthearts.org.
- **The Directors Guild of America (DGA):** The DGA offers information on contracts and legal rights for directors. Website: www.dga.org.
- **FilmLawyers.com:** This is the resource for finding legal help specifically tailored to the needs of filmmakers,

including contracts and rights issues. Website: www.filmlawyers.com.

## Location Scouting and Permits

- **Film commission websites:** State film commissions provide information on filming locations and permits. (Search for your state's film commission online.)
- **Location Managers Guild International (LMGI):** This website offers resources for location managers and scouts, including guidelines for obtaining permits. Website: www.locationmanagers.org.
- **Peerspace:** An online marketplace for booking unique spaces for film shoots. Website: www.peerspace.com.
- **Giggster:** A platform for renting various locations for filming. Website: www.giggster.com.

## Postproduction Resources

- **American Cinema Editors (ACE):** Resources for finding editors and understanding the editing process. Website: www.ace-filmeditors.org.
- **The Post Production Handbook:** A detailed guide covering various aspects of post-production. (Available at bookstores and online.)
- **The Dailies:** A platform that helps manage daily shoots and review footage efficiently. Website: www.thedailies.com.

- **Free music websites:** Resources like Free Music Archive, Epidemic Sound, Artlist.io, and YouTube for sourcing royalty-free music. Free Music Archive: www.freemusicarchive.org. Epidemic Sound: www.epidemicsound.com. Artlist.io: www.artlist.i. YouTube Audio Library: www.studio.youtube.com/channel/UC6qQ0R8gDqRO6R6DrcpDlGg/music.
- **Freesound.org:** A collaborative database of Creative Commons licensed sound effects and audio samples. Website: www.freesound.org.

## Film Education and Training

- **MasterClass:** Offers courses from renowned filmmakers and actors, covering various aspects of filmmaking, including writing, directing, and acting. Website: www.masterclass.com.
- **Coursera:** Provides online courses on filmmaking from accredited institutions, covering topics like screenwriting, film production, and editing. Website: www.coursera.org.
- **No Film School:** A community and resource hub for filmmakers, offering articles, tutorials, podcasts, and forums. Website: www.nofilmschool.com.

## Film Festivals and Competitions

- **FilmFreeway:** As mentioned earlier, this platform allows filmmakers to submit their work to thousands of film festivals. It's a great way to get exposure and feedback. Website: www.filmfreeway.com.
- **Withoutabox:** An online submission service for filmmakers to submit their films to festivals, with a focus on independent films. Website: www.withoutabox.com.

## Funding and Grants

- **The Film Fund:** Offers grants for short films and features, with a focus on emerging filmmakers. Website: www.thefilmfund.co.
- **Women in Film Finishing Fund:** Provides grants and financial support for women filmmakers completing their projects. Website: www.wif.org.
- **Sundance Institute Grants:** Various funding opportunities for independent filmmakers through grants and programs. Website: www.sundance.org.
- **The Black List:** A platform that helps screenwriters and filmmakers connect and promote their work. Website: www.blcklst.com.

## Distribution Platforms

- **IndieFlix:** A streaming platform that focuses on independent films, providing filmmakers with a way to distribute their work. Website: www.indieflix.com.
- **Vimeo On Demand:** Allows filmmakers to sell or rent their films directly to viewers. Website: www.vimeo.com/ondemand.
- **FilmHub:** A distribution platform that connects filmmakers with streaming services and digital platforms for wider distribution. Website: www.filmhub.com.

## Production Services

- **Film Riot:** A website and YouTube channel offering tutorials, tips, and gear reviews specifically for indie filmmakers. Website: www.filmriot.com.
- **Cinevate:** Provides gear and tools specifically designed for filmmakers, including sliders, tripods, and rigs. Website: www.cinevate.com.

## Marketing and Promotion

- **Social Media for Filmmakers:** Online courses and resources on using social media effectively to promote films. Website: www.socialmediaforfilmmakers.com.
- **Film marketing resources:** Websites offering strategies and tips for marketing indie films, including blogs,

webinars, and downloadable guides. Website: www.filmmarketing.com.

## Film Equipment Rental

- **ShareGrid:** A platform for renting film equipment from local filmmakers, making high-quality gear accessible to indie filmmakers. Website: www.sharegrid.com.
- **LensRentals:** An online rental service for cameras, lenses, and other production equipment. Website: www.lensrentals.com.

## Connections and Mentorship

- **Film Fatales:** A networking group for women filmmakers, providing support, resources, and connections. Website: www.filmfatales.org.
- **Local film festivals:** Many local film festivals have mentorship programs, networking events, and workshops for emerging filmmakers.

## Business and Contracts

- *The Business of Television* by Ken Basin
- *Hollywood Dealmaking: Negotiating Talent Agreements for Film, TV, and Digital Media* by Dina Appleton and Daniel Yankelevits

## Links I Used in My Cold-Email Outreach (Chapter 17)

- Selina Ringel stand-up set:
  https://vimeo.com/366381005
- *Tuning In* trailer (miniseries on Amazon):
  https://www.youtube.com/watch?v=9mGbQlpqxq0
- *The Best People* first feature trailer:
  https://www.youtube.com/watch?v=lhlxdakbOlY

These resources can significantly streamline the process of finding crew and talent for your projects. Whether you're looking for experienced professionals or emerging talent, these platforms provide various tools and networks to help you build your filmmaking team effectively.

• • •

Additionally in this Resources section, I'm providing the **budget** and **schedule** for our first feature film, *The Best People*, to give you a sense of how we allocated resources on a project made for under $150,000, as well as how we structured the timeline.

I'm also sharing the **investor deck** for *You, Me & Her*. While I've removed the financial details because your film's requirements will differ, this is the exact deck we used to secure our angel investors. It was effective for us, so it might be helpful as a road map as you create your own investment deck. Remember to adjust it based on your tone, comparable films, and financial needs.

I've also included some **poster designs** from three of our projects, along with a brief analysis of each. Creating posters has always been a challenging process for us—it typically takes a month or two before we feel confident about any option. My husband has a good eye for design, but we both go through multiple iterations before settling on a final choice.

**Poster 1: *You, Me & Her***
**Genre Indications:** The relaxed beach setting, soft color palette, and casual attire of the characters suggest a romantic drama or romantic comedy. The composition, with characters sitting closely but facing different directions, hints at a potential love triangle or complex relationship dynamics.

Design Analysis

- **Color Scheme:** The sunset and sandy beach create a warm, inviting feel, aligning with romance or lighthearted drama.
- **Typography:** The clean, minimalist font and the spacing around the title convey a modern, indie vibe, appealing to an audience that appreciates character-driven stories.
- **Character Arrangement:** The three characters shown in a beach setting, with direct gazes and relaxed poses, suggest intimacy and possibly tension, giving viewers a sense of personal connection within the storyline.

**Effectiveness:** This poster works well because it visually captures a sense of calm and introspection while hinting at relational tension. It's likely to attract viewers interested in complex relationships and emotional narratives.

**Poster 2:** *2 Moms 1 Mic*

**Genre Indications:** The bright pink background, colorful toys, and playful poses immediately suggest a comedy, likely a stand-up or family-related comedy special. The title *2 Moms 1 Mic* and the prominent microphone reinforce the stand-up theme.

## Design Analysis

- **Color Scheme:** The vibrant pink background and primary-colored toys add a fun, playful feel that aligns with comedy, especially family or parenting humor.
- **Typography:** The large, bold font is quirky and a bit distressed, giving a casual and approachable vibe, appropriate for a comedy special that doesn't take itself too seriously.
- **Character Positioning:** The two women, seated with children's toys, are posed as if they're about to deliver a comedic routine. Their expressions are lively and engaging, which suggests humor and relatability.

**Effectiveness:** This poster effectively communicates its genre at a glance and is likely to attract parents or fans of relatable, family-centered humor. The colors and lighthearted imagery make it stand out as a feel-good, fun experience.

**Poster 3: The Best People**

**Genre Indications:** The formal clothing, wedding setup, and the tagline "They want to tie the knot? We think not." suggest a romantic comedy with a twist, possibly focusing on unconventional views on relationships or marriage.

## Design Analysis

- **Color Scheme:** The soft peach background with hints of white from the wedding setup keeps it light and comedic, yet sophisticated.
- **Typography:** The clean, modern font and subtle underline under "people" provide a contemporary feel, appealing to audiences that enjoy smart humor.
- **Imagery:** The characters' poses—two appearing unhappy, one couple in love, and a burning wedding bouquet—suggest conflict and comedy around romance or marriage. It gives a clear visual cue of the film's plot without revealing too much.

**Effectiveness:** This poster effectively balances humor with sophistication, appealing to viewers who appreciate romantic comedies with a critical or comedic twist on traditional marriage themes. The unique setup and burning bouquet create curiosity about the storyline and tone.

* * *

What follows are some fun behind-the-scenes photos from various projects that I've written, produced, and primarily starred in! My husband, Dan, directed all of these projects. While I have worked on many other projects, I believe these particular ones best represent me as the train driving each endeavor forward. I've also included the "first texts" for a couple of projects, which show what it actually looks like (at least in my world) to start from the proverbial idea on a napkin.

Performing my dream stand-up comedy special, *2 Moms 1 Mic*, at The Virgil was a career highlight. In these photos, you'll see me on stage and with Kaela Crawford from our photoshoot during the live taping. We held two performances that night, each with over eighty people in the audience. We filmed both shows, later intercutting them to create the final comedy special. We achieved this entire production with a total budget of just $10,000, capturing the energy of a live crowd. We got to live the dream of making our $300,000 Netflix comedy special without $300,000 or Netflix. Achieving our dream—and by dream I mean the feeling you get by being present in the moment you had always imagined—was the biggest reward of all of it, and learning to enjoy that and feel the dream is a big part of true success.

## *2 Moms 1 Mic* Stand-Up Comedy Special

Selina Ringel
selinaringel

OCT 24, 2:37 PM

I started writing a new half hour set that I want to record early next year. It's going to be all mom material for the most part and then I thought maybe you'd want to do something like that with me! We each do half hour sets and so then combined we have an hour special and call it 2 Moms One Mic  or something mom themed! Totally just a thought and no worries if this is not something you want to do!!!

♡

I would love this!!!!

This sounds so fun!! I have so much material just need to get it in a better place but maybe we can help each other out ? Lol

## *Single Mother by Choice*–Behind the Scenes

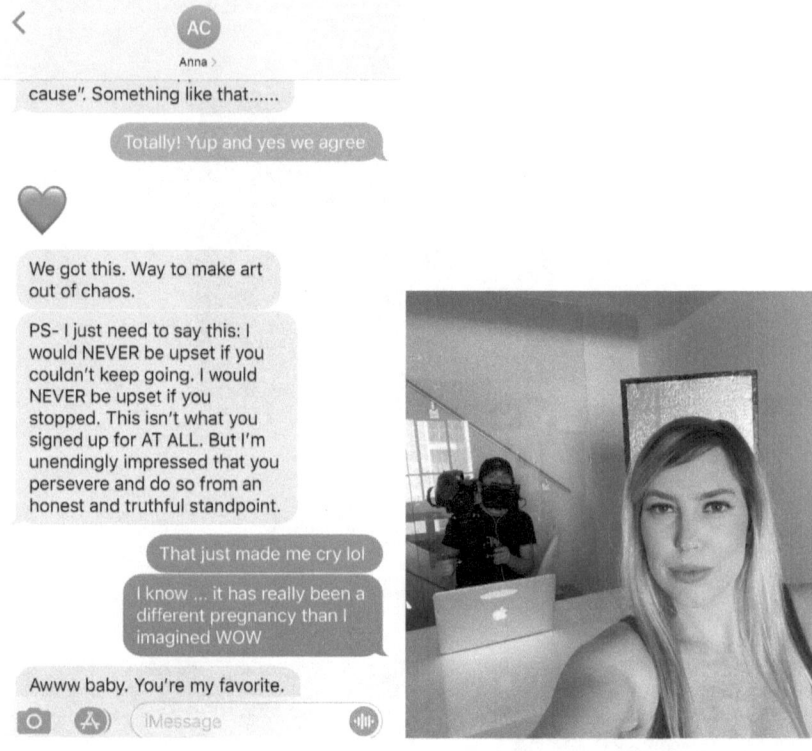

This behind-the-scenes shot gives a glimpse into the creative and resourceful approach we took for *Single Mother by Choice*. We organized a socially distanced press photoshoot on set, arranged interviews, and even set up a DIY press space at home. It's a testament to how much can be accomplished with determination and a hands-on approach.

## *The Best People*-First Feature Film BTS

Behind-the-scenes photos from *The Best People*, our first feature film, reveal the heart and effort that went into bringing this project to life. Working with a limited budget, we made every moment on set count. These images capture the raw energy of our team as we embarked on our filmmaking journey, learning to maximize resources while pushing creative boundaries.

### *Tuning In*-Digital Series BTS

Our series *Tuning In* provided another opportunity to experiment with storytelling on a modest budget. These behind-the-scenes shots show us in action, embracing the challenges of a smaller production while focusing on authentic performances and impactful moments. Every scene was a chance to grow and learn, as we continued honing our skills and refining our vision.

## *You, Me & Her*-Enhanced Production Value

Behind-the-scenes photos from *You, Me & Her* reveal how the production value has significantly evolved across our projects. A production assistant was even holding an umbrella over me to shield me from the sun as I walked to my scene. In the early days, we could never have imagined having enough crew on set for this kind of VIP treatment. It made me feel like an A-list star—which, while it might sound silly, felt really rewarding and reminded me that our sets are growing. The difference is evident in each image, showcasing the growth in quality and polish over time. No matter the budget, it's always possible to bring your vision to life—just keep giving yourself permission to dream big and continue creating!

# OUTLINE

What follows in this section is the original outline for *Single Mother by Choice*, which was originally titled *37 Weeks*. You might gain added insight by watching the movie on HBO Max alongside this "original" version and comparing it to what ultimately appeared on screen.

The pandemic forced us to rewrite the story, but even under normal circumstances, scripts evolve—from outline to screenplay to final edit. Flexibility is essential in filmmaking, but so is knowing when to set firm boundaries to preserve the elements that matter most. This balance of adaptability and focus is crucial for navigating the inevitable changes while staying true to the core of your story.

## MONTH 1
### (Pgs. 1-11: Opening Image, Setup, Theme Stated)

- Eva prepares for her birthday party, juggling work and personal messages. She drafts and sends a text to Felipe.
- Skye, her free-spirited roommate, is upset about Eva planning her own party. Skye agrees to handle the cake.
- Eva runs errands and stresses over her busy workday.
- At the surprise party, Felipe doesn't show. Skye brings out a psychedelic cake, encouraging Eva to go with the flow (Theme Stated). Skye later reveals the cake has mushrooms.
- In a hallucinatory haze, Felipe shows up. Eva awkwardly lets him in, leading to an implied conception scene.

## MONTH 2
### (Pgs. 12-25: Catalyst, Debate, Break Into Two)

- Eva takes a pregnancy test, unsure of the result. Skye jokes about it and helps Eva buy more tests.
- After multiple tests and a doctor's visit, Eva learns she is pregnant but with low HCG levels, leaving her unsure about continuing.
- Eva plans an abortion but reveals past trauma to Skye. After a heartfelt moment, they decide to face the pregnancy together.

## MONTH 3
### (Pgs. 25-40: B-Story, Fun and Games)

- Eva refuses to slow down, juggling work, exercise, and her new management company.
- She and Skye bond over their quirky friendship but clash when Eva spots and worries about the pregnancy.
- A humorous doctor's visit highlights their unique relationship, with the doctor assuming they're a couple. Eva texts Felipe, who ghosts her.
- They share a touching moment at the first ultrasound.

## MONTH 4
### (Pgs. 40-55: Fun and Games)

- Eva and Skye's friendship strains as Eva becomes pregnancy-obsessed, while Skye prioritizes her personal life.
- They reconcile before the second ultrasound and celebrate hearing the heartbeat.
- A trip to Joshua Tree strengthens their bond after another fight.

## MONTH 5
### (Pgs. 55-65: Midpoint-Reversal of Fortune)

- Eva and Skye visit Eva's controlling parents. Eva resolves to be more patient and adaptable.

- At a gender reveal party, Eva starts working on self-improvement and letting go of control.

## MONTH 6
## (Pgs. 65-75: Bad Guys Close In)

- Eva feels isolated as Skye focuses on her girlfriend. Eva loses a client and spirals emotionally.
- In a jealous rage, Eva confronts Skye and her girlfriend. The confrontation ends with Eva experiencing a pregnancy scare and going to the hospital, where she learns she must rest.

## MONTH 7
## (Pgs. 75-85: All Is Lost, Dark Night of the Soul)

- Skye plans a chaotic baby shower, leading to a heated argument. Skye announces she's moving out.
- Eva is left alone and begins preparing the baby's room, processing her emotions.

## MONTH 8
## (Pgs. 85-95: Break Into Three)

- Eva bumps into Felipe at the grocery store. He apologizes for ghosting her and offers support.

- Eva finally accepts help, signaling her emotional growth.
- Skye sends a heartfelt video, showing she's still there for Eva in her own way.

## MONTH 9
## (Pgs. 95-100: Finale)

- Eva gives birth, with Skye visiting in a silent, heartfelt moment. Felipe arrives with his girlfriend, creating a bittersweet scene.

## MONTH 10
## (Pgs. 100-110: Final Image)

- Months later, Eva embraces her new life as a single mother and successful business owner. She's calm, present, and content, with Skye as the baby's godmother.

**MESSAGE:** True happiness lies in letting go of control and living in the present.

**QUOTE:** "Beware of destination addiction . . . happiness will never be where you are until you give up the idea that it's somewhere else."

# BUDGET

What follows in this section is a "top sheet" (overview) of how we allocated resources for a micro-budget feature film.

We worked with SAG actors under the SAG Ultra Low Budget Agreement and used a most-favored nation payment model for department heads. Initially, we planned to make the film with $30,000 and equity-based compensation, but we ended up raising more funds due to growing enthusiasm.

Notably, this budget excludes delivery and marketing costs—something I now highly recommend including. After three features, I've learned that finishing a film is just the beginning; setting aside funds for visibility is crucial.

Visit **www.bethetrain.com** for the full breakdown.

## TITLE: THE BEST PEOPLE

Producer: SELINA RINGEL
Director: DAN LEVY DAGERMAN
Dated: 10.4.16
Location: LOS ANGELES, CA
Script Dated: 10.2.16
Budget Draft
Start Date: 10.17.16
Finish Date: 11.5.16
Total Days: 17 DAYS
Travel Days: 1 DAY

| ACCT# | CATEGORY DESCRIPTION | PAGE | TOTAL |
|---|---|---|---|
| 1100 | SCRIPT | 1 | 1,400 |
| 1200 | PRODUCERS UNIT | 1 | 5,000 |
| 1400 | CAST | 1 | 12,000 |
| | | Total Above-The-Line: | 18,400 |
| 2000 | PRODUCTION STAFF | 5 | 9,600 |
| 2100 | EXTRA TALENT | 5 | 1,600 |
| 2200 | SET DESIGN | 6 | 4,800 |
| 2400 | SET DRESSING | 6 | 2,500 |
| 2500 | PROPERTY | 7 | 1,500 |
| 2600 | SPECIAL EQUIPMENT AND ANIMAL | 8 | 200 |
| 2700 | WARDROBE | 9 | 3,500 |
| 2800 | MAKE-UP AND HAIR | 10 | 2,400 |
| 2900 | SET OPERATIONS | 10 | 7,120 |
| 3000 | GRIP | 11 | 3,520 |
| 3100 | ELECTRICAL | 12 | 3,400 |
| 3200 | CAMERA | 12 | 10,400 |

| 3300 | PRODUCTION SOUND | 13 | 4,525 |
|---|---|---|---|
| 3500 | LOCATION EXPENSES | 14 | 10,128 |
| 3700 | LOCATION TRANSPORTATION | 15 | 530 |
| | Total Below-The-Line Production: 65,723 | | |
| 5000 | EDITORIAL | 17 | 2,900 |
| 5100 | MUSIC | 17 | 3,900 |
| 5200 | POST-PRODUCTION SOUND | 17 | 5,000 |
| 5700 | ANIMATION & VISUAL EFFECTS | 17 | 1,000 |
| 5800 | VIDEO POST PRODUCTION | 18 | 2,000 |
| | Total Below-The-Line Post: 14,800 | | |
| 6500 | PUBLICITY | 19 | 1,500 |
| 6600 | INSURANCE | 19 | 6,508 |
| 6700 | GENERAL EXPENSE | 19 | 275 |
| 1500 | FEES & CHARGES | 19 | 1,384 |
| 6900 | ADMINISTRATIVE EXPENSES | 20 | 250 |
| | Total Other-Below-The-Line : 9,917 | | |
| | Contingency: 6.0% : 6,769 | | |
| | Total Below-The-Line Other: 6,769 | | |
| | Total Above-The-Line: 18,400 | | |
| | Total Below-The-Line: 97,209 | | |
| | Total Above and Below-The-Line: 115,609 | | |
| | Total Fringes: 3,979 | | |
| | Grand Total: 119,588 | | |

# SCHEDULE

What follows is the first day of the shooting schedule for *The Best People*.

We filmed for a total of fourteen days, taking a break every six days. In addition, we had two dedicated B-roll days in Las Vegas. I also made sure to include one reshoot day in the budget, which I highly recommend. You never know where your movie may go or if you'll need to tweak something, and having an extra shooting day in the budget can be a lifesaver. Keep in mind that the number of shooting days has a direct impact on your budget.

For example, on day one, we shot six pages plus 7/8 of another page. When scheduling, it's helpful to plan your heavier shooting days earlier, so you have room to shift anything you didn't finish. It's common advice to aim for three to five pages per day if this is your first time shooting, as everything tends to take longer than expected. However, be sure to consult your first assistant director, who helps keep the set on track, and your line producer to determine what's realistic for your project.

The typical shooting day lasts twelve hours, plus a lunch break. Lunch usually begins when the last person in line receives their food, and the break can range from thirty minutes to an hour, depending on what the director and cinematographer are trying to achieve with the lighting. Any time worked beyond this schedule is considered overtime, which is charged separately for both the crew and the actors.

Factors like the number of shots, locations, scene complexity, and scene changes all influence the schedule and budget. It's important to allocate extra time for key emotional scenes—rushing through these can be detrimental. If you have the opportunity to work with professional actors, rehearse well in advance and ensure they are off-book (i.e., know their lines). This will set you up for a smoother schedule.

Visit the Resources page at **www.bethetrain.com** for the full schedule.

**CAST MEMBERS**
1. JOE
2. ANNA
3. CLAIRE
4. CLAIRE (O.S.)
5. ART
6. ART (O.S.)
7. JOHNNY
8. JOHNNY (O.S.)
9. VANA
10. KYLE
11. CHARLEY
12. MARIA
13. MAX
14. ALBERT
15. BRAD
16. TRAVIS
17. JEFF
18. OLDER GUY
19. MAKE-UP ARTIST
20. JEROME
21. JOHNNY'S MOM
22. MODEL 1
23. MODEL 2
24. OTP (O.S.)
25. SARAH
26. SEXY LADY
27. HAIR STYLIST

# THE BEST PEOPLE

SCRIPT DATED—SEPTEMBER 7, 2016
REVISED SCHEDULE—SEPTEMBER 9, 2016
EQUIPMENT PICK UPS—OCTOBER 14, 2016

| \*\*BEGIN PRINCIPAL PHOTOGRAPHY- OCTOBER 17, 2016\*\* \*\*DAY ONE- MONDAY, OCTOBER 17, 2016\*\* | | | | | |
|---|---|---|---|---|---|
| Sheet #: 3<br>1 pgs | Scenes:<br>4 | INT Day | CLAIRE'S APT - LIVING ROOM;<br>CLAIRE tries to comfort ANNA<br>and they decide to go to KY. | 2, 3 | Est. Time<br>Ivana's<br>Apartment |
| Sheet #: 11<br>1 pgs | Scenes:<br>7 | INT<br>Morning | CLAIRE'S APARTMENT;<br>ANNA walks in and looks at<br>old photos of her and Claire. | 2 | Est. Time<br>Ivana's<br>Apartment |
| Sheet #: 131<br>3 pgs | Scenes:<br>11 | INT Day | CLAIRE'S APT - LIVING ROOM;<br>CLAIRE and ANNA continue to<br>talk about JOHNNY. | 2, 3 | Est. Time<br>Ivana's<br>Apartment |
| Sheet #: 34<br>1 1/8 pgs | Scenes:<br>20 | INT Day | CLAIRE'S APT - LIVING ROOM;<br>CLAIRE walks in with a huge<br>smile, ANNA is annoyed. | 2, 3 | Est. Time<br>Ivana's<br>Apartment |
| Sheet #: 57<br>1/8 pgs | Scenes:<br>36 | INT Day | CLAIRE'S APT - LIVING ROOM;<br>ANNA gets a text from ART. | 2 | Est. Time<br>Ivana's<br>Apartment |
| Sheet #: 130<br>1/8 pgs | Scenes:<br>9 | INT Night | CLAIRE'S APT - LIVING ROOM;<br>ANNA takes some pills before<br>crashing on the couch. | 2 | Est. Time<br>Ivana's<br>Apartment |
| Sheet #: 32<br>4/8 pgs | Scenes:<br>19 | INT Night | CLAIRE'S APT - LIVING ROOM;<br>ANNA swipes through<br>BUMBLE. She texts CLAIRE. | 2 | Est. Time<br>Ivana's<br>Apartment |
| **END OF SHOOTING DAY 1 - MONDAY, OCTOBER 17, 2016**<br>**6 7/8 PAGES** | | | | | |

# INVESTOR DECK

The images in this section are from the investor deck for *You, Me & Her*. Please note that investor decks can vary greatly depending on the type of movie you are making. Visuals are crucial—they help convey the tone of your movie and showcase comparable titles, giving investors a sense of what to expect while highlighting what makes your film unique and a "must-make" project.

It's important to remember that while you can never guarantee investors their money back, it's essential to have confidence in your project's potential to succeed financially. Build your deck with the investor's perspective in mind: if you had disposable income and a love for movies, would this deck convince you to invest?

Focus on what makes your deck professional and exciting. What elements make it hard for an investor to say no? Ensure your presentation reflects the effort and thought you've put into the project. When it's clear that you're prepared, committed, and capable of following through, investors will feel confident that you deserve their support and will deliver a great film.

As we continue to develop and package this film (which is premiering shortly after this book was sent to the printer), we are constantly revising our deck. Things can change frequently—actors may drop out or join, or additional funds may be raised—and it's important to keep the deck up to date. By treating our investor deck as a living, breathing document, we ensure it reflects the evolving momentum and current status of the project.

# YOU Me AND HER

## Introduction

It's fair to say everyone in a long term relationship has fantasized about what it would be like to be with someone else. Some people cheat and lie but what if as a couple there was a loophole?

What if all it takes to be someone else is to include someone else?

## Logline

On their first trip to Puerto Vallarta after having a baby, Magdalena ('Mags' Mexican-American) and Ash (Indian-American) attempt to rekindle the spark in their marriage but can't help arguing the whole vacation until they meet Angela, a spiritual digital nomad that takes a romantic interest in Mags. Suddenly Ash and Mags start to reconnect over the idea of having a menage a trois.

The stars don't align, but when they return home to their jobs and their baby, Mags receives a text from Angela asking if she can crash at their house for a few days. They accept in hopes that the excitement of the potential sexual experience will save their marriage.

**LANGUAGE:** Spanglish

## Theme

Assumptions about our significant others and ourselves stop us from being happy and exploring who we truly could be.

## Characters

### MAGDALENA

Magdalena "Mags" Chandra-Ramirez grew up in Mexico with a Mexican father and an American mother; she's Latina but looks as white as can be. A new mom that is a Type-A, obsessive planner, she is the breadwinner of the family because she manages her family's commercial real estate firm. She lives her life in a box and doesn't like to color outside the lines. She doesn't trust that she can count on anyone to do what she does so life has become about taking responsibility for everything. She's a know-it-all but somewhere deep down she's lost and has no idea who she is or how to find herself.

**CAST:** Selina Ringel

**CAST:** Ritesh Rajan

## ASH

Asheem "Ash" Chandra-Ramirez, Mags husband, an Indian/American, late 30's dreamer who has yet to find success and that's developed a chip on his shoulder. He doesn't know it, but he's having a mid-life crisis. He's a creative entrepreneur whose cannabis app is on the verge of blowing up and he's starting to celebrate a little early. He loves smoking weed and wants more than anything to be a boss in his life and to provide for his family and is so excited to prove to everybody that he's going to be able to do this through his passion for cannabis.

## ANGELA

A care free yoga instructor and spiritual guide that leads yoga and mindful meditation retreats all over the world. She's been through the ringer and finally landed at spirituality to deal with it all. Emotions come in waves and she knows that no human nor emotion will tie her down to anything. By allowing herself to be open to everything she always remains free.

**CAST:** Sydney Park

## MARIMAR & ALVARO

The perfect couple.... Or so it seems. The hotel owner and his influencer lover that Mags and Ash meet at the hotel in Mexico.

**CAST:** Roberto Aguirre & Marianna Burelli

## BEN

A frat boy turned lawyer. Ash's neighbor and friend who's become closer since they started their weekly trivia night tradition and recently helped Ash with a contract for his first cannabis client.

CAST: Adam Ray

## INVESTMENT OPPORTUNITY

- The first payout goes to investors until 100% of their capital investment is recouped by them. The investors will get a 20% preferred return on 100% of their capital investment.

- After the investors recoup their initial investment and preferred return (20%), the Director and Writers will be paid as they are not paid out of the production budget and have agreed to defer their pay in the interest of reducing the cost to produce the film.

- After the investors and deferrals are paid, the receipts from all sources of revenue are split between the investors and the production company 50/50. The production company split consists of percentages given to the director, producers, actors, writer, etc.

- On the investment side, your individual investment reflects the percentage of the film you own; in this case 100% of the investor's side of the series, for the life of the film.

- This is a passion project; as such, the writer/producer/star and director/producer will not be taking up-front fees from the production budget, and are seeking in-kind contributions to reduce the budget.

- Our last film SINGLE MOTHER BY CHOICE doubled our investment on the film's sale to HBO Max.

## CAPITAL RAISED

**Capital raised to date** (production is already greenlit):

**Minimum capital to greenlight project** (good production):

**Target Budget** (great production):   | **seeking $**

**Target Budget** (ideal production):   | **seeking $**

*\*\*Projected returns on the next slide\*\**

*Bio*

Two Hands Productions is an award winning production company led by husband and wife team Dan Levy Dagerman and Selina Ringel.

Their most recent feature film SINGLE MOTHER BY CHOICE told a fictional story which tracked Selina's real life pregnancy during the pandemic. The film sold to HBOMAX and won Film Threat's Award This! For Best Indie Drama and Best Director of 2022.

Their first film THE BEST PEOPLE was acquired by Samuel Goldwyn Films and is available on Amazon Prime and all over the world.

## OUR TEAM

### SELINA RINGEL, Writer/Producer/Star

Selina Ringel is a Mexican American award winning actress, comedian, writer and producer. Her most recent feature film, SINGLE MOTHER BY CHOICE, a hybrid docu-narrative that tracked her actual pregnancy in real time during the 2020 pandemic, is streaming on HBOMAX. Selina recently finished filming her first stand up comedy special 2 MOMS 1 MIC with Kaela Crawford. Selina graduated with a Masters in Fine Arts from the Producing program at the AFI Conservatory in 2014. She and her husband run their own production company, TWO HANDS PRODUCTIONS.

### RITESH RAJAN, Producer/Star

A graduate of NYU Tisch, you can see Ritesh's work as the lead in Sujata Day's new film DEFINITION PLEASE produced by Mindy Kaling & Ava DuVernay, as Farran in the Emmy award winning hit RUSSIAN DOLL and as the voice of Ken in BARBIE: DREAM HOUSE ADVENTURES and more all on Netflix. Other credits include recurring on Shonda Rimes STATION 19, Disney's THE JUNGLE BOOK, Freeform's STITCHERS, NCIS LA, STAR WARS REBELS, BEAVIS & BUTTHEAD and the Hulu original, DOLLFACE.

## OUR TEAM

### CAMERON FIFE, Producer

Cameron works as a producer, production manager, and director, freelancing for various media and production companies. Recently Cameron has worked on comedy specials for Netflix, CW, F/X, and Hulu, as well as the indie feature Definition Please, released on Netflix in January. His background is in the theatre, and while his skills include line producing, creative producing, directing, script writing, development, budgeting, accounting, scheduling, production management, and post-production supervising, anyone who knows him can say with one hundred percent assurance that he's a dancer first.

## OUR TEAM

**IRREVERSIBLE PICTURES, Production Services (Mexico)**

Irreversible Pictures is a company specializing in the production of top-of-the-line feature films and scripted TV series. They also offer production services for every level of film and series project in Mexico, and the U.S. They're based in Guadalajara city, México, and in Los Angeles, California.

They have produced movies and series in both English and Spanish language for a large number of clients and companies, including Netflix, Amazon Prime, Sony Pictures, Studio Canal, Pantelion (Lionsgate), Pantaya, Videocine (Televisa cine), Mira Vista, Corazón Films, Gussi Artecinema and others.

## OUR TEAM

**DAN LEVY DAGERMAN, Director**

Dan received his MFA in Directing from the AFI Conservatory. Dan's second feature SINGLE MOTHER BY CHOICE, a fictional feature that tracks his wife's real life pregnancy in 2020, premiered on HBOMAX last year and won BEST INDIE DRAMA and BEST DIRECTOR at Film Threat's Annual AWARD THIS! show in 2022. His first feature film THE BEST PEOPLE won the Special Jury Prize for Best Comedy Feature and Best Supporting Actress at WorldFest Houston and was distributed by Samuel Goldwyn and sold worldwide by Shoreline Entertainment. Dan has directed several other award winning productions: OUR NEED FOR CONSOLATION (starring Stellan Skarsgård), REAL LOVE (starring Christy Romano), and SOLILOQUY, which have screened at festivals all over the world including Palm Springs Shortfest, Gothenburg Film Festival, Mill Valley. Dan is a partner in Two Hands Productions with his wife Selina Ringel.

## LOCATIONS
*(MAG'S HOUSE, SOUTHERN CALIFORNIA)*

# SAN PANCHO

# LOCATIONS
(THE RESORT)

# LOCATIONS
(ANGELA'S SAN PANCHO)

# LOCATIONS
(NATURE)

## COMPS

**THE OVERNIGHT**

BUDGET: $200,000
BOX OFFICE: $1,110,522

**THE ONE I LOVE**

BUDGET: $100,000
BOX OFFICE: $596,933

**YOUR SISTER'S SISTER**

BUDGET: $125,000
BOX OFFICE: $3,324,070

**BRITTANY RUNS A MARATHON**

BUDGET: 1M
BOX OFFICE: $3,324,070

**CELESTE & JESSE FOREVER**

BUDGET: $200,000
BOX OFFICE: $3,640,975

BUDGET NUMBER ASSUMPTION IS THAT THESE REPRESENT "BELOW-THE-LINE" EXPENSES (HARD COSTS)

## Contact

TWO HANDS

| Selina Ringel | Dan Levy |
| --- | --- |
| [Phone Number] | [Phone Number] |
| [Email Address] | [Email Address] |

## ABOUT THE AUTHOR

Selina Ringel is an award-winning writer, producer, actress, and entrepreneur whose work includes three feature films, a comedy special, and a digital series.

Her first feature, *The Best People*, was sold to Samuel Goldwyn Films (MGM) and distributed in over forty countries. She shared an Award This! honor for best indie drama of an independent film for her second feature, *Single Mother by Choice*, which was sold to HBO. This movie earned back double its investment, which is an incredible feat in independent film. Her stand-up comedy special, *2 Moms 1 Mic* (with Kaela Crawford), and the digital series *Tuning In* are both on Amazon Prime. Her third feature, *You, Me & Her*, has a 100 percent score on Rotten Tomatoes and has won fourteen awards. It will be distributed through a first-of-its-kind partnership using cutting-edge technology to connect filmmakers and producers directly with theater owners.

Over a fifteen-year career, Ringel's scripts have won or been finalists at Slamdance, WIF, and the Blacklist, and she has been a guest judge for festivals such as Film Outside the Frame and Tilt Up. She is a graduate of AFI's MFA producing program and runs her own production company, Two Hands Productions, with her husband and business partner, Dan Levy Dagerman.

www.ingramcontent.com/pod-product-compliance
Lightning Source LLC
LaVergne TN
LVHW041921070526
838199LV00051BA/2697